FOREWORDS BY
Bishop Reg Piper & Rev Jonathan Shanks

Tell Them
I'm Alive

HEARING FROM GOD THE UNEXPECTED

Marion Estelle Brown

Ark House Press
PO Box 1722, Port Orchard, WA 98366 USA
PO Box 1321, Mona Vale NSW 1660 Australia
PO Box 318 334, West Harbour, Auckland 0661 New Zealand
arkhousepress.com

Unless otherwise stated, all Scriptures are taken from the New Living Translation (Holy Bible. New Living Translation copyright© 1996, 2004, 2007, 2013 by Tyndale House Foundation. Used by permission of Tyndale House Publishers Inc., Carol Stream, Illinois 60188. All rights reserved.)

Some names and identifying details have been changed to protect the privacy of individuals.

Cataloguing in Publication Data:
Title: Tell Them I've Alive
ISBN: 978-0-6489912-3-6 (pbk)
Subjects: Biography
Other Authors/Contributors: Brown, Marion Estelle

Cover photo: "Boots" in Charcoal by the author.
Design by initiateagency.com

For my grandchildren Della, Judah & Sophie
When I first set off on these journeys you were very small. It was the hardest thing to say goodbye, but I knew the best I could do for you was to obey God.
Now each one of you know Jesus for yourself.

CONTENTS

Thank you

Priscilla & Gordon Griffiths

for gladly reading and editing my manuscripts
and encouraging me to keep writing.

FOREWORD

Abraham was seventy-five when God called him to leave country and kindred and go to a land that God would show him. Moses was eighty when God called him to leave his father-in-law's flock and lead Israel out of Egypt. Why was I surprised when God so obviously laid upon the heart of a single woman, "a widow" of a mere sixty plus years, a passion to help some of the most vulnerable people on earth.

Marion was a member of the congregation I was serving. She was, in her words 'an ordinary parishioner'. I knew her as one with her own share of joy but also pain in discipleship. It was in these very struggles that the Lord Jesus was teaching her dependence and perseverance. He was preparing her to undertake an extraordinary task. She was to be an everyday follower of Jesus living at times in volatile contexts.

In very fluent writing Marion tells the stories of the people she met and prayed for, of the heart-wrenching sadness she came across, of the difficult situations she encountered and of both the respect and hatred she experienced as a foreigner. In all these situations she writes of the way God called upon her to demonstrate the kindness of the Lord she served. She had to deal with the disappointment of a new ruling of the organisations that managed the projects in which she was involved. In considering workers' safety no more short-term mission could be undertaken in danger zones. To her own surprise opportunities opened up to go to new fields to serve, with the same passion to show Christ's love.

You will enjoy the easy style, the stories and the inner thoughts Marion reveals of her walk with Christ. If you are like me, you will be amazed at what she attempted through Christ. She felt compelled to tell people who were imprisoned by circumstances, trapped in misery and hemmed in by grief and spiritual darkness, that Jesus the great Liberator could not be incarcerated even by death. He was alive and ready to free all who wanted that freedom.

Bishop Reg Piper
Formerly Rector of Gymea Anglican

FOREWORD

Marion turned up to the church I was pastoring in Sydney a little 'shell shocked' and in need of encouragement. I would later realise it was I who would be encouraged. She told me of her heart for the Hazara people of Afghanistan. She had a distinct call from Jesus to stand with the women, casualties of war.

A few months later she asked my thoughts on her taking into her home a young male Afghan refugee making a new life in Australia. My standardised "safe" pastoral response didn't seem to work on Marion. She walks to a slightly different drumbeat.

Over the next few years as her pastor I began to be greatly encouraged by this passionate mature woman. Her unmasked authenticity and love for Jesus, and for people, in that order was infectious and challenging.

It is an absolute privilege to read her story "Tell Them I'm Alive". I couldn't put the book down, enthralled by the back story of the adventures with Jesus this brave grandmother has undertaken.

In a world where risks are increasingly avoided, Marion recounts a testimony of trusting and obeying, loving and forgiving, risking and rescuing.

This is a story about never giving up on the promptings and call of God. Marion, thank you for once again inspiring and encouraging me to listen to and love people in Jesus' name. And if I get the chance I too will "Tell them He's Alive".

Rev. Jonathan Shanks
Senior Pastor,
Northern Life Baptist Church

PROLOGUE

Like many, I enjoy listening to, or telling a story. So often it is around a meal, or shared with a trusted friend. Sometimes we are given brief intervals to swap stories, small anecdotes but don't get to hear the whole of the tale. Perhaps this is why friends have urged me to write a book. They wanted to hear a bit more. So here it is.

I was retired and loved being a grandmother when life took a different turn. My family were moving away out of our city. I loved spending time with my grandchild and helping my daughter with another little one just three months old. It was then, reflecting on how I would miss them when they moved away, that I asked God:

"What do you want me to do now?" There were many needs around me, and being one of simple, practical expectations I imagined it was something close to hand.

"Women casualties of war" came the words into my spirit and mind.

"Where Lord?" I asked Him.

"Afghanistan" came the answer.

It came as a puzzling suggestion. It seemed strange, even alarming.

I tested this word with mature leadership in my church. They seemed surprised and curious but were willing to help me. I was encouraged to follow through with enquiries.

It was suggested that a wise preparation was to qualify as a teacher of English to Speakers of Other Languages. It was considered a well-accepted and useful qualification for entry into difficult locations.

I spent the next few months going to university, sitting in a windy bus stop shelter late at night after lectures, imagining and wondering what lay ahead. I researched the people most in need in this troubled land. I was connected with those who were already working in Afghanistan and increasingly grew in eagerness to join them.

With my qualifications in teaching English completed I applied to a respected mission organisation and progressed through their training course. At a final interview for being accepted into short-term mission, I failed. I was raw and ill-prepared. It was decided I wasn't overseas mission material. I was advised to wisely stay at home and work with Afghan women refugees in our city. I needed to accept I wasn't sufficiently resilient.

I let my email friends working in Afghanistan know I wouldn't be arriving as we thought. They were disappointed because they were looking forward to me coming. So was I.

In a regional city of Sydney I came to delight in teaching my Afghan women friends for that is what they became. I also listened to their stories of trauma of loss and displacement and was moved to pray with them often. I saw their determination to overcome. Our English lessons became lively and interactive. I had the joy of seeing their confidence growing in speaking English, while wrestling with our complex grammar. In my final days of teaching them, they decided to sing for me a traditional Afghan song. Percussion was tapped in rhythm on their desks. They swayed and sang, breaking into laughter as a finale. Over these two years I visited two families in their home and became entwined in their lives and they in mine. That is a story all of its own.

When this season closed I wondered what next? It was now well over three years since trying to figure out what God intended for me of a longer-term nature if anything. After many months, and hoping I was by now a little more resilient, I made cautious enquiry of another overseas mission organisation. They responded with enthusiasm. This particular organisation had no work in Afghanistan but instead asked me would I be prepared to go to Pakistan, where there were many Afghan refugees. I said "*Yes*".

By now I knew for certain, it would only be possible as Jesus gave me the strength of His presence and direction. I would need to lean on Him with fresh purpose. This is where this story begins.

It is a chronicle of continuing to hear God and what He determined to do. I hope as you read you can come with me. This is surely you, wherever you are, as a follower of Jesus. I know you too will be endeavouring to follow Him, in your unique place, at home or somewhere else. Trust in our heavenly Father is a powerful challenge for any of us who love Him.

I want you to come with me, and walk in my shoes, or boots as they often were. For the sake of God's kingdom sometimes our feet are called to walk in very surprising places.

Some are just 'under our nose', others require awkward change, even what appears for a time, as unreasonable. But it is our Father's kingdom He is building. His call, on His terms.

I hope you are encouraged to take fresh steps in faith, knowing we are in the company of our gloriously risen Christ. The one who came in human flesh, yielded to a scornful and despicable death on a cross. In those hours, the one who was perfect, took the punishment for our sin before God and rising from the dead now resides in human form in glory. In His resurrection power we are able to overcome our own inadequacies or fears fuelling reluctance.

If you as yet don't know Jesus, nor believe there is a God, stay with me. Or perhaps you know about Jesus, and even accept He was a true person come to earth, but as yet do not know He wants to relate to you personally. Perhaps you did believe in Him once, but your heart and courage has been broken. Let me tell you, He has never let you go.

I pray you may come to the knowledge you are loved more than you could imagine. You are of such value to the One who made you. Jesus died for all the perplexing issues for which you may never have found an answer, where life has brought loss or disappointments or betrayal for which you were unprepared. If you have experienced injustice, He knows the rage still lodged in your soul. God knows why you have sought comfort outside of Him. May this story be a healing for you.

Jesus knows the deep cry in your heart for which you have no words. Not only did He die for you and for me He overcame death for us to know His presence, His security, and why He made us for His purpose for eternity.

As we are given a gift of faith to acknowledge His death for us, and surrender to the risen Christ, we will know for certain His unfailing love, His eager forgiveness, His protective shelter, His mindful provision, His gracious mercy.

PART 1
2010

1.

UNKNOWN

Coming through the exit door of the arrivals lounge at Lahore airport in Pakistan, I looked into a sea of brown eyes. Hundreds of them. I heard a voice call my name and an arm reaching to attract my attention. It was my host for the next two days. Dust and pollution clouded the lights in the airport carpark. Could anyone breathe in Lahore? In an old second-hand car, we met the city traffic head-on. Cars came up on our left, pressing their horns just making the clearance of our mudguard. My host pressed her hand on the horn, her foot on the accelerator, defying cars, trucks, motor bikes and a donkey pulling a load. I burst out laughing in alarm. This was Lahore traffic at midnight?

I knew little of Pakistan, except what I had learnt on our nightly current news reports in Australia. I knew the Prime Minister Benazir Bhutto had been assassinated three years before. I knew there were ongoing issues with surrounding nations, but little else. What I did know was that Pakistan still welcomed Christian workers; those who respected and honoured the cultural and political and religious restraints. Originally a part of India, two separate nations were created in 1947. India, as majority Hindu, while Pakistan was established as an Islamic Republic. The first to do so.

The organisation I was registered with in Australia, had not sent anyone to Pakistan for many years. A cluster of photocopied notes issued by the organisation was all I had. From those few pages I was prepared for how to dress and to greet as well as being very careful where possible, not to offend the Muslim believers. I understood how Christian workers from many nations over many years, had established hospitals and schools. All with the intention of showing the people of Pakistan the love of Jesus.

I was untravelled outside of Australia except for one brief holiday to a Pacific island many years earlier. That time I was with others.

Before arriving in Lahore to the midnight traffic, I sat in the waiting lounge in Bangkok for my flight. I was engrossed in a book. For a moment I looked up. A host of Pakistanis, men, also waiting for their flight, had their eyes fixed intently on me, a foreigner, and a woman. I had no head-covering, so quickly realised my dress didn't qualify as acceptable. I swiftly gathered my things and took refuge in the ladies room, to don a scarf to cover my head, and a shawl around my shoulders. Returning to the waiting lounge, I took up a seat with my back to the crowd. An older silver-haired Pakistan gentleman came and sat one seat away, but next to me. It was a careful gesture on his part to protect me.

I had yet to learn, a woman alone, particularly an older woman is a puzzle for locals in Pakistan. I needed to defend myself as a widow being alone. In true terms according to our law, I was a divorcee. For the sake of Pakistan's culture, I was to be considered a widow. Within their culture an older woman without her husband or family, for any reason is hardly acceptable. I was yet to learn how important this is for them, as I was to be asked more than once, "Where is your husband?" For now, I was alone and waiting to take a flight to the unknown.

The engine revved and shuddered into full throttle. The voice asked for seats to be upright position and safety belts locked. The stewards sat in their appointed seats as the Airbus moved out of the boarding space and turned to find the runway. I was the only western woman among the couple of hundred passengers returning home or visiting relatives. I was seated next to a family and smiled at the child next to me sitting on her mother's knee. The pilot waited for clearance and so did we.

No one around me looked at all familiar. I thought of my family, my small grandchildren. There were now three. I thought of my faithful friends, my brothers and sisters in my church. All had prayed for me when I was sent off. Some were praying for me right then I was sure. They knew my flight times and connections. The clearance came and again the engine revved for power and moving down the runway, gathering momentum, lifted off, swaying and rising, gaining altitude. I was afraid. No turning back now.

It was a fear washed with joy. I was finally on my way to where I'd been focusing and praying and preparing to go for many months. I plugged in my music and heard the words "Grace upon grace, flows down". I whispered "*Thank You*" to Father God many times over until we could undo our safety belts and relax. Four and half hours to Lahore. I did not know the breadth and depth nor height of what 'grace upon grace' would encompass. I soon would puzzle, laugh, query, ponder, struggle, in wonder and surrender to instalments of the unknown and unpredictable. Jesus was about to surprise and challenge me. In relinquishment of what I wanted he would give me His desires of my heart.

As Christians in Pakistan we are not allowed to initiate evangelism but are able to answer truthfully the reason for our faith, if questioned by those who seek to know. We can explain our faith but not with a view to persuading anyone. It meant that as foreign workers we are dependant entirely on God. He is the one who opens up opportunity. He knows those who are truly hungry to come to faith in Jesus, His Son.

2.

JOURNEY TO RAHIM YAR KAHN

For the first five days in Lahore I attended a conference for new workers to Pakistan. When it closed, I took a 10-hour coach trip to Rahim Yar Khan, where the headquarters of our organisation was centred. It is a regional rural city 600 Kilometres to the South. We joined the modern highway which runs from Islamabad to Karachi. Traffic moves fast. Australian eucalypt trees in many parts line the road. It was a great introduction to some of the Pakistan countryside. Broad sweeping acres of cotton or grass filled the landscape. Stretches of land were ploughed and lay fallow. A brick kiln belched smoke at a distant view and donkeys pulled heavy loads on a dray. I sat in the front seat next to the bus steward which meant I had for 10 hours a panoramic view of Punjab farm life. Coach stops were unique.

We were photographed and scanned for weapons and our hand luggage searched.

The same had occurred on boarding in Lahore. I was told this does not normally happen, so there must have been a security alert that day. I could hardly have been a threat to public safety as twice the young stewardess fell asleep on my shoulder. She supplied us all with a cool drink at intervals. When the driver noticed I was stretching my legs to ease cramps, he asked me would I like to sit on a seat normally folded against the wall, near the front steps, with ample leg room.

He gave me a warm farewell when the bus pulled into Rahim Yar Khan and wished me well. It is very important in Pakistan to honour a guest, a visitor. I sat waiting in the closing hours of light to be picked up.

My English host and hostess for the next three days, chatted warmly, taking me through the city of Rahim Yar Khan, down the busy thoroughfare. In the night light donkeys sauntered or waited for the next slap of leather to move. Motor bikes came in metal speed, and bicycles dodged a frantic car horn, or goats being herded through the shopping centre.

"*This is authentic Pakistan!*" my host lovingly chanted. It was a boast I would come to understand. Nowhere else that I went to in Pakistan was quite like what I saw that first evening and the days following. It is a moving picture in Rahim Yar Khan that accommodates and nurtures the ancient and the modern, as if two movie-sets had somehow got mixed up. No-one thought it was odd. It is strangely wooing. I came to love and puzzle. Moses with a mobile?

I was fast asleep in my host's guest room. when a wail of a scream broke my deep sleep.

I leapt out of bed and went to the window, to figure who might have been attacked, only metres from my bed. I heard footsteps retreating up the laneway. I looked at my clock. It said midnight. In the morning I questioned my host.

"*Oh sorry, we should have told you*" he said. "*That's the street crier going around to check that all is well. The scream tells us that we are safe. We sleep through it. For us it is just normal*". I must have slept through it the next night, unless he found a different laneway to assure others they were safe.

After a few days in my hosts' home, it was time now to settle into my own space in the organisation's headquarters. It was situated in a leafy square of colonial homes, around a parkland. Streets still have English names, dating from the time of British colonial rule. The local Christian church is also housed in this complex. It is guarded 24 hours by Pakistan police who have their own watch-house near the gate.

I was registered with the local Police, who must be informed on movement from city to city.

The first morning shopping on my own for food, a well-dressed man followed me on a slowly driven motor bike. I later recognised him as a plain-clothes policeman who regularly came to check in at the watch house and was reassured it would be because I was new and needed protection.

I had opportunity to chat with one of the watchmen. He asked me questions about my life and why I was in Pakistan. He shared about his family and his plans. He was engaged to marry a young woman in his hometown many kilometres away and was missing her. Most painful was the loss of first his mother, and four months later, his father. This was all in the few months before he and I were speaking. He was a young man in sorrow. I asked him could I pray for him to Jesus who I believe in?

He eagerly said:

"*Yes please*". He was calmed in his soul after this and said:

"*Thank you*". We talked often and he asked me many questions. It became a valuable friendship.

Close by the small unit I lived in, was the workshop for the Vocational Program which was a means of giving young men from Christian families living in rural poverty, prospects for employment. They were being trained in tailoring. If after twelve months they qualify, they are given a manual sewing machine and an amount of money to either be employed in the marketplace or set up their own business. They are taught about Jesus and the most delightful songs of worship. Their training workshop backed onto my living quarters and early around 8.00 am, their voices in worship rang out into the morning. It was beautiful. It so often set my focus for the day.

I came to chat with them regularly, in gestured English in their workshop. I was intrigued that they sat cross-legged at a low wooden bench. They turned the wheel by hand to set the speed for the needle on their manual sewing machines. These are distinctly Pakistani sewing machines, glossy black with gold decorative writing and scrolls. They reminded me of the old Singer treadle machine on which I learnt to sew as a child.

They were always eager to show me their latest tailoring. We talked about young men in 'my country'. They really wanted to know. I explained among other things, surfing, enacting a surfer on a surfboard, ducking and rising to balance in a wave. Skateboarding I found a bit more difficult. It's possible I have permanently ruined the image of both for them. They threw their heads back laughing. We became smiling, waving, hello friends, as I saw them every day. Over the mobile, they sang for my son-in-law in Australia, who I explained sang worship songs too. They and he were thrilled. Their Pakistani rhythm is catchy and their voices robust. On Sundays the Pakistan Christian Fellowship whose church is also in the building filled the air with the same distinct sound of Psalms in Punjabi.

3.

ALL THINGS BRIGHT & BEAUTIFUL

While my main intent was to go north to Islamabad, the capital of Pakistan to teach Afghan women refugees, I agreed with a request to first come for this month's stay to teach English at the Allied Model School. The students ranged from kindergarten to around Year 7 and Year 8. I needed to be driven to the school through the hectic traffic. No allowances are made for pedestrians by donkeys, rickshaws, motor cyclists, cyclists, nor by cars, and in some moments, a camel.

The school was sheltered from the commotion of the main street and tucked down a quieter lane near a wide-open space. Building rubble covered the ground to the entrance. The School was being re-built from two small classrooms to one of two-levels with several classrooms. For this season, classes were combined, and some students sat out in the courtyard under the sun. Special consideration was given to me when a single room was made available to me and each cluster of children processed into what, for as long as I was teaching, was the English Room. It was an organizational challenge particularly as I had to make great effort to understand the staff's limited English and they, my gestured English and complete lack of Urdu. They were very patient.

The School was established many years ago by missionaries, for educating poor children from Christian and non-Christian backgrounds. In 1972 under Zulfiquar Ali Bhutto (Benazir Bhutto's father) all Christian schools and colleges were nationalized. While the school is unapologetically Christian, a certain quota of Muslim staff is mandatory. The rest are Christian. Discretion is needed as overt proselytizing is against the law. I did however, open each lesson with prayer to our Father God, committing our time together into His hands. At the end of the lesson I prayed for the children, committing them to Him. "*That they might come to know what You are really like Father. That they would come to know just how much You love them*". I made every effort in my lessons to teach them that He made them, and He loves what He has made. I prayed that even my face would tell the children they were loved.

I was moved to tears sometimes over individual children as I sensed their need. The students looked at me attentively, hungry to learn. Pakistan children are highly regimented in school. Not once in the weeks I was there did I need to reprimand or rebuke a child. Occasionally their teacher rebuked them, but only exceptionally. They are brought up by their parents and grandparents to esteem teachers highly. It was an honoured place I was given.

No tables for teaching notes or resources existed. Every ounce of available seating or surface was used. The school was very simply furnished, particularly while in building mode. Very few students had the luxury of a desk to write on, but instead, balanced a clip board on their knee. Any available desks were put in the English Room for some of the children to write their English. It was a generous gesture to me. They made every effort out of very sparse resources to provide what I needed.

I made the children laugh or smile at each other over me, as I attempted to wear the mandatory *dupatta* (head covering). I could take it off my head to teach but had to keep it over my shoulders. It felt like having two disabled wings flapping around and getting in the way. I would wrap it around my throat some mornings to stop it flapping. I almost succeeded in strangling myself one day when I caught one end of it in the zipper of my bag. None of this was missed on the children and a gentle murmur of laughter could be heard.

Because all my resources were on the floor every time I bent over to retrieve them, or a truant piece of chalk, my *dupatta* would fall over my face and for a moment when I stood up, none of the students could see my covered face. In one exasperated moment I got it and shoved it in my bag, telling it to *"stay there!"*. The students in the front row of desks broke into laughter which was wonderful. Fortunately, it was my last lesson, so grace would have been given I'm sure. I would have been older than most of the children's grandmother, or in some cases great-grandmother. I loved making them laugh.

I also enjoyed seeing their delight at being given coloured felt pens for creating the most unique pictures. Their absorption in the novelty of using brilliant colour, created a perfect silence in the classroom. On the first lesson to give them the pens, when I said the lesson was finishing, no heads looked up. They didn't hear me. They were so far-away enjoying. I looked at the teacher, a Christian. He smiled in wonder, looking lovingly at them, gently shaking his head seeing their pleasure. Turning to me: "*Thank you, thank you, ...SO happy*".

I let them continue until their closing bell and slipped out of the room to go home. My pick-up driver would be waiting. It made me wish that felt pens would never run out. They would not be able to afford having those purchased for them by their family. There were essentials needed in the school before coloured pens. They experienced for just a few simple hours, deep and rich colour coming onto their page. They were very proud of their artwork, and after other lessons stood up in front of class and spoke out the learnt English phrase for the day to describe their picture. It was a joy to be there in those moments. These and the older student's artworks were expressions of the theme of my English lessons, the ancient hymn: "*All Things Bright and Beautiful*".

In an update to home, written from Rahim Yar Khan when it was time to say good-bye, I wrote:

> '*I completed my time at the School this week, hopeful that most of the children had grasped the predominant vocabulary and essence of "All Things Bright and Beautiful". I told them again and again that God made them and loved them. One's heart could break as the truth of God was listened to with intense dark eyes hungry to learn. A collection of their drawings and words collated into each individual book, was handed out on the last day. All 160 pupils rewarded me with a rendition of "All Things Bright and Beautiful" so joyously sung I thought the walls might fall in! They*

laughed and laughed out of sheer impish delight at their volume. So did I, along with the teachers. It was fun! One little girl as the children were filing out of the classroom, broke rank and stretched up her arms to give me a hug. The staff are committed to keeping the song in the school's repertoire which is so rewarding.'

The preparatory and first-class children had earlier in the week, created colourful birds, butterflies and flowers with an assortment of sparkling paper and glue. These were suspended from the low ceiling in two classrooms. The joy created in their construction was encouraging. Pakistan children are heavily regimented as a rule, but for two glorious hours, the floor was covered in sparkles and tiny hands brought me their works of art amidst spontaneous chatter.

The teachers presented me with a cluster of roses and special morning tea to say, "*thank you*". I was grateful for their trust and patience with me.

To my brothers and sisters back in my home church in Australia, I wrote...

'Your prayers are deeply effective. I am so grateful to you as you remember the context I am in. There is undoubtedly a battle for these children's lives. It has been hard some days'

On returning home to Australia I received an email from the leader of our organisation in Pakistan which provided a postscript to my days in the school. The end of year Christmas programme gave opportunity for two of the senior girls to sing a duet of "All Things Bright and Beautiful.' The postscript said:

'It has to be said that the tune had become slightly modified with rehearsals but was still recognisable and the words were beautifully clear. Wish you could have been here'.

Bearing in mind that while a few of the boys in this school come from remote areas, from Christian families, most of the students come from local homes, following the major religion. We need as believers to pray for the Christian teachers under deep restraints; that when the good news is legitimately taught at Christmas and Easter, that the Holy Spirit will birth faith in the students.

4.

CHANGE OF PLAN

It was arranged that after spending this month in Rahim Yar Khan I would travel to Islamabad where there was a college for Afghan refugee young men and women to learn English. In that same year when my travel and work plans were being laid, Pakistan experienced a catastrophic flood. The mighty Indus River which flows from the Tibetan Plateau down the length of Pakistan to the Arabian Sea burst its banks in the torrential rain. Twenty million people were displaced. Homes and crops destroyed for hundreds of kilometres southwards.

Mission staff all over Pakistan left their appointed tasks and went to help in relief work. They came from all areas. The staff at Murree Christian School in the northern mountains beyond Islamabad, rallied. Teaching was continued there with a skeleton staff and adequate provision made for the children. Other workers attempted to come but were stranded waiting for the floodwaters to subside. Volunteers who could travel, camped in the villages still standing, distributing food and supplies.

By the time I arrived in late October, the waters had receded, and daily trips were being made to the victims by the organisation's team officially appointed for flood relief. I was eager to go on at least one trip if possible. This was granted to me and my trip was a day I will never forget. It opened my eyes to suffering on a scale that is hard to grasp. Travelling southward great cavities metres deep could be seen with shells of homes teetering on the abandoned edges. No sign of communal life was left. What had once been a community of homes with families, was no more.

After this initial trip the team asked me would I please go again. I did, gladly, and it was made possible by tailoring times with my English teaching to suit the School's needs. Except when occasionally one of the wives could go, it was an all-male relief team. To have a woman in the team meant the women in the villages had someone to relate to. Women in Pakistan cannot congregate with men and must stand afar off when the men queued for the supplies. It was one of the unexpected blessings that I was able to accompany the team on several trips, travelling long distances into the Southern Punjab. On other days we travelled further on south, crossing the border into Northern Sindh province.

The team usually comprised the team leader, a delightful Chinese brother who gave the orders which we all had to obey swiftly. This was essential on the days we were in hostile territory where crime had broken out. Default plans were quickly put in place where potential danger was sensed. Often an Ethiopian brother, an eager evangelist would join the team. On other days we would pick up a local pastor in the affected area, so he could accompany us to distribute to his people. An intense eloquent Pakistani brother interpreted and explained much to me. We were driven by a professional Pakistani driver whose skill on the road I came to respect. My life depended on it.

Sitting in the front passenger seat next to him in the four-wheel drive, he refused any expression of anxiety, so there was to be no pressing my foot suddenly on the floor in imaginary braking. He didn't think he needed to brake. I think the oncoming load of hay taking up most of the narrow country road, might have thought he did! I have never laughed so much out of nervousness. I think he enjoyed making me scared. It became a game and finally, I was not afraid. I trusted his God-given skill and was at peace. We became the firmest friends. On the long return trip home late at night, when the preacher and the interpreter had gone quiet, I kept him company chatting in simple English phrases to help him keep awake.

"*Good teacher, very good teacher*" he affirmed. They were rich days of mission shared. The first of these trips to bring relief, was to a weary flood-ravaged community in the Punjab region.

5.

CORRIDORS OF DUST

I looked down a corridor of dust and rubble, heaped in tidy piles of bricks, stones and timber. Here, all that was left of a valley of homes after the merciless floodwaters had receded. A little girl put her hand in mine and begged me to come, pointing down the valley. Other children gathered and agitating, followed closely. We walked down the slope, through foundations of what had once been their secure place. Past blue tents, we ducked and wove our way through washing on lines propped by leaning posts. Children pulled me to show me what had been their home, another pile of bricks. Stale melancholy hung in the dry heat of this community as fathers and mothers individually called from a distance in their language to me. It was a plea to view their pile of bricks.

Grief makes a weary face, some silent, simply looked, asking. One confident girl took me to where her father, uncles, cousins and brothers had already begun to rebuild a very solid brick dwelling. It was still uninhabited, waiting to be completed. It promised safety and warmth for the winter to come and a shelter from the searing heat of summer.

Holding a child's hand, I began walking, returning the way I had come. I intended re-joining the relief team further up the slope, when I was invited to sit down on a chair salvaged from the chaos of dusty remnants. I was handed a book covered in dried mud, with many pages stuck together, from the floodwaters.

It appeared to be a book for teaching English to young Urdu-speaking students. The child who brought it wanted me to read it aloud to the crowd that had gathered around me. I searched and found a story of a dove that had brought a stick to rescue a drowning dry-land creature. I wondered if it was a story more for me, rather than them. The child persisted urging me to read it aloud. It was almost cruel in its relevance for a people who might not understand. Few would have understood the English text.

I was overcome by the heat and clamour of the crowd of children and mothers compacted around me. Little light was left to read the print. I begged them to move back and they shouted to each other to do so. The story I was reading was a puzzle for these people left destitute by the flood. I stopped and wondered whether reading it was at all helpful, if in fact they could understand it. I knew on one occasion a dove depicted the Holy Spirit, but they didn't know that.

The crowd had increased and surged around me again to shut out the light. I finished reading the story and stood up to breathe more air. I could now see the elders of the community had come to see what was happening. The men on the edge of the crowd, were agitated with intense angry enquiry at me in their faces. I needed to be wise. I lifted my hands to heaven, looked upwards then closed my eyes.

A power surged through me. I believe it was the Lord's strength as I prayed in a heavenly tongue as safeguard against being accused by them and held to ransom. I had been warned that kidnapping occurs in some places where people are desperate and hostile. A pastor's son had been kidnapped the week before but released after an all-night vigil was held. Only the Lord of heaven would know what I was asking. I knew He knew. The heavenly tongue gave place to a whispered plea in my own tongue for Father God's mercy for them, I asked Him for a revelation of His Son to come to this community.

A voice higher up the valley called out; "Come! Come!" A woman close by me instantly took my hand and pulled me through the crowd and we ran, hand in hand, breathless through the dusty foundations, the piles of bricks, ducking the washing, through the corridors of remnant walls and up to higher ground. The relief team sensed an urgent need to be off for our safety.

I was told later that World Health Organisation had endeavoured to bring relief provisions to this people but refused to get out of their vehicles so great was the anger and hostility of the men in the community. A sad report, but one I realised highlighted God's mercy and unique protection to His servants. Our relief team had been able to stay for this length of hours without incident.

God put it on one man's heart in this community to ask our evangelist:

"Please come and tell us about your God". A weekly bible teaching and worship service began, but was soon challenged by authorities, which was a disappointment. Kingdom pursuits are made by travail, and through setbacks. The Lord has heard our prayers for this people.

6.

ROOM IN THE DARK

The room was lit by one distant electric bulb. Natural light lit up just part of the room coming through a window and doorway looking out onto a porch. The rest was dim to dark. I tried to adjust my vision and sat on the bed alongside my fellow worker. We had come to visit a young widow. Her husband had died just 10 days before. She gazed at us looking for help. Her head-covering was casting added shadow over her face. I was disturbed for her so not speaking her language I prayed quietly in whispers for her. My companion was close to her and held her hand, she spoke quietly and comfortingly in Urdu..

The children gathered in the room, all girls. They pressed themselves closely against us as if proximity might help us to know what to do. The young simply stared. I hugged a child standing near me and prayed. Another came and stood very closely, expecting a hug They moved and jostled, coming close to receive a hug each one. They were curious and intent, just looking, whispering. Slowly others shouldered them for a place close to me. I held each

ROOM IN THE DARK

one in turn and prayed. My eyes gradually adapted to the dim light, so I could make out faces more clearly. The children smiled coyly, but it was still shadowy, as an old woman came in to see what was going on. The girls chatted and giggled without sound and spoke something to her.

The old woman moved up to me very earnestly, bent over and holding her face close to mine, peered into my eyes as if she was finding it hard to see me. She spoke something in her language. Perhaps it was a greeting or a question, I didn't know.

There was agitation in her leaning so closely. It was such a fearful look in her face, a darkness in its intensity. I was repelled. I spoke words of plea to Jesus, as a protection. The darkness in her face was frightening. Her eyes and her grimace were ugly. I spoke whispered words:

"Your blood Lord Jesus speaks for me". We both needed Him. I stood up and put my arms around her and as I held her I said:

"Jesus loves you. He loves you. Jesus...." It was a prayer of begging Him to overrule the power of the evil I saw in her. She smiled as if she was pleased with whatever I had spoken. I believe she felt the welcome and warmth of Jesus's love. She was at peace after that. Later, before leaving she allowed me to take a photo of her in the courtyard, calmly holding the hand of the daughter of my team companion, I think the family around her noticed a difference. She was at peace. The agitation and darkness had left her.

Being welcomed into this family belonging to the majority religion, was made possible through one young man. This one son in his twenties, who had given his life to Christ, witnessed to his brothers and sisters. Our evangelist and his wife continued regular visits to this household, teaching and explaining the gospel.

7.

FATHER'S MERCY.

On a gentle rise in the same town, was a Hindu community who had suffered extensive damage from the floodwaters. I was welcomed into a home, where a baby just 10 days old, was fast asleep, wrapped in a simple swaddling cloth. I looked above, and only a few inches from the sleeping babe, the wall was leaning precariously towards it. Great splits in the clay had been wrought under the pressure of the flood waters. I covered my mouth with a gasp! I was imagining the wall could easily collapse on the child. I expressed this through our interpreter, but the family were not perturbed. They explained it was the coolest place to put the babe to shelter it from the intense heat outside. I placed my hand on the sleeping child and prayed for God's protection. I prayed that this child would be set aside for Christ's kingdom, a little girl, someday a woman, in God's grace and mercy, kept for His purposes.

Outside in the sun, was a boy, who I was told was 8 yrs old. He lay on a raised camp bed, out in the hot sun. It was explained to me through translation that for three years he had lain prone, not able to sit up. He could not speak but was completely paralysed. He had to be spoon-fed, without any ability to use his arms or hands. He once was a happy boy running around but was stricken with a sudden illness and had never recovered. I asked through interpretation, could I please pray to Jesus for him? With the family's permission I then got up onto the camp bed and cradled him in my arms. I prayed for God's mercy and healing virtue to rest on him. I prayed too that he would have a revelation of Christ into his heart and mind and soul. I then lay him back on his bed. Joining with me, in that prayer was my Ethiopian sister in Christ.

The head of this household was a Hindu Guru. God's hand was on this family. I sensed His grief for all that they had suffered. I was given a piece of traditional embroidery worked by the Guru's wife. It indicated their gratitude for my praying for their son. The Hindu Guru asked our Ethiopian teacher and his wife, would they please return and tell them more about Jesus?

8.

HEAVEN SPEAKS URDU

The day was already promising to be hot when we left the organisation's headquarters in Rahim Yar Khan, for another village distribution of food and household items. The supplies were going ahead of us separately. We travelled through the little townships of bazaars and shops selling everything from fruit and vegetables, meat hanging waiting to be carved on selection, to hats and jewellery. Sometimes the shop is also the workshop and craftsmen are visible.

A furniture maker was busy in his opened workshop with fine chairs and assortment of small tables arranged on the ground below. His workshop was elevated, and could have been a stage. It was an intriguing performance. Others were arranging metal pans and cooking articles, or farm instruments out for display. It was an ever-moving theatre. Old men, and those with no work sat smoking and drinking chai.

Sweeping is a favourite activity in Pakistan. Dust is on everything, unless it is swept that is. Often traffic was held up in these small townships, so the four-wheel drive we travelled in had to slow down, pause and finally stop and wait. It usually meant a donkey with an enormous load had stopped or was going too slowly for cars and trucks to pass. I loved these interludes as it gave me time to take in the detail. More than once I went to get my camera, but we were off! The donkey had moved to the side and horns and shouting resumed full pace, too soon to capture it.

As is customary, when we arrived at our determined village for distribution, the men on the team attended to the farmers waiting. This time the supplies had arrived ahead of us. In a tent erected as a shelter from the intense heat, the husbands and fathers began receiving the supplies of food. Many had lost their livelihood after the critical, damaging flood. Most crops in these surrounding regions had been destroyed. These were families without food.

I walked towards the homes nearer shade, where a dozen or so women stood under the nearby trees. It was well within the proximity of their homes. These were dwellings not destroyed in the flood. This cluster was built in a horse-shoe shape on a gentle rise. Goats nibbled on the scant grass, and dogs lay in cool spots. In customary hospitality the women retrieved a rattan couch-bed and laid on it a quilt and cushions, moving it under a tree for me to sit on. I smiled and said in Urdu:

"*Thank you*" They chatted to me and looked in wonder. Usually when interpreted for me in other places, they were commenting on my white hair or age, along with phrases of "*welcome and rest*". The children had by now gathered around us.

The women stood around me, very closely, smiling.

"*Engelesee*" I was telling them I spoke English. They smiled and nodded that they understood and brought me a cool drink. The heat had intensified and the cool drink refreshing. There is kindness in so much of Pakistan culture for a visitor, however poor or lacking, they give generously and eagerly. Not knowing their language there was only a hug I could give with a grateful heart. I reached out to the woman closest who seemed the leader of the group.

I spoke the word "*Jesus*". I wanted to hug her for Him. I sensed His love in my heart, His compassion. As I held her, I prayed for her. When she moved away, she turned to her women friends and echoed the word "*Jesus*" chattering something in her own language.

Each woman came holding out their arms for what she had received. As each turned away she repeated the word "*Jesus*" that she had heard. One by one, they stretched out their arms to be held and spontaneously uttered the word "*Jesus*" in echo after me. It spread like Chinese whispers as more came asking for a "Jesus". Some came for a second and a third "*Jesus*". Some came for a fourth time reaching out their arms, speaking His name in request. I could not speak Urdu, but heaven does, and I hugged the women and children for Jesus' sake. I asked for His mercy and love and grace to meet their deepest need. I believe Jesus did come. I sensed very clearly His presence and comfort for them.

The heat was so intense the women led me to the shade of a porch in the home on the rise ahead. Again, bringing out a rattan couch and laying a patchwork quilt and a beautifully embroidered pillow, they invited me to lie down. They connected a huge electric fan to blow cooling air over me. Such was the loving spontaneity of their respect.

One of the women went quickly to a close-by neighbourhood to call a friend to come and meet me. I looked up from a drowsy sleep by the fan, to see her face peering in urgent anticipation at me. She opened her arms and received a "Jesus" hug. In a little while, the interpreter and I walked back to her village with her for a cool drink. At her invitation, he explained the gospel to her. She responded by telling us her husband was away working in a distant location when the torrential rain began. She and her children became fearful. She had called out to God when they saw the floodwaters rising around their home.

"God has heard me" was her response to us.

Our interpreter and I walked back to where the distribution of grain and supplies was completed. The men came to a patio area just near the porch in which the women sat. The elder of the community invited our preacher-teacher to speak. With men numbering about 15 to 20 and about a dozen women, the One in whom we believe, was explained from the scriptures. It was an attentive group. God had opened a significant door for His truth to be heard among this Hindu community.

The young woman from the neighbouring village who had watched the floodwaters rising around her home, whom the interpreter and I visited, rang him many times in the following weeks. She asked questions of the truth he had shared. She was able to attend regular talks which now take place in her village. The Bible Society established a Culture Centre there, giving opportunity for the villagers to become literate in their own language, with the ability for them to study the scriptures for themselves.

9.

GIFTS

One of the delights in Pakistan was the light in the eyes of those who believe in Christ. They sparkle like jewels in a dark place. The darkness is palpable. One such collection of jewels is a rural Christian community; a hard-working people in the southern Punjab. They are surrounded by neighbours following the majority religion, An outcome from the flood was the accessibility to, rather than isolation from these Muslim neighbours. Walls of prejudice in the past between neighbours were torn down. Opportunity came for the Christians to give relief in a time of destitution, and their Muslim neighbours to receive in their humbled state. The Christians were able to bless those who might have been alien to them.

Our relief team brought water filters to offset disease breaking out since the flood, as well as warm quilts for the winter, along with winter clothes. We brought these on a number of days to the home of a pastor who with his sons and nephews, and brothers gave gladly to those who came. Names of families were called out from his written list. Their home was a distribution centre for miles around. This continued for some months as the relief team took truckloads of provisions to them and others. Muslim neighbours who received relief from them, acknowledged to the Pastor: "*Your God is with you!*"

On one distribution day we drove the pastor to one such neighbour, down near the Indus plain, a sweeping majestic space that had been totally covered in the flood. We sat under a canopy erected on an elevated spot. I watched the neighbour's face, weary and broken. There was nobility in his thankful expression to his Christian neighbour, for the gift of the essential water filter. He and his sons smiled at me to include me in their gratitude. It was a fragile moment for them.

The children who came with their families for relief, were so easy to love. They were dusty and their clothes covered in the dirt of many days. I hugged them again and again. It became a game. On one subsequent visit, they recognized me as we got out of the four-wheel drive and they ran towards me, raising their arms for a hug from me, boys and girls and tiny tots. On one such day when all the children had been hugged one little boy asked our interpreter:

"*Can we hug her?*" I sat on the ground so they could easily reach me and one by one they put their eager arms around me, their dirty hair in my ear and snotty noses against my neck. Their unwashed skin was silken against my cheek. They held me for a long moment. One tiny tot rested his head on my shoulder and stayed. How precious they are to Jesus. I have given each one to Him for His keeping, for His salvation. Mothers and babies likewise have been prayed for, so many of them so young.

10.

UNEXPECTED

Little did we know that just a fortnight later, we would be back in this believers' community, sitting with and comforting them in the loss of one of their young men. He had been active in the distribution of water filters to the surrounding neighbourhood. Our Ethiopian brother told me the family were refused a burial of his body in the local burial ground, because he was a Christian. The bodies must be buried before sun-up the next day. Our brother in Christ sat in the back of a truck, nursing the young man's dead body, weeping as they travelled many kilometres in the dark night hours, to bury him in an acceptable place.

Neither did the Pastor's wife know that day when she had welcomed us so warmly that her much loved sister would die suddenly. The young man passed away on the Friday. Her sister on the following Wednesday. Death comes swiftly and cruelly to them. As God's beloved sons and daughter's these believers had come into "the valley of the shadow..."

As a team we returned when we heard the sad news of both passing. I sat with the Pastor's wife. As I held her hand I could sense the presence of the Lord in her, deep in grief for her. Her precious sister had died the night before when the community was still shaken by the death of the young 19 yr. old man.

For a long time, she and I just sat, holding each other's hand. At intervals I prayed quietly for her, but chiefly just sat. After time, through the interpreter I gently told her in simple quiet phrases that I too, had lost my sister. I told her I remember thinking *"I don't know how to live without her"*. She nodded and tightened her grip on my hand. A long time passed and we simply sat. The hours passed. Dusk was setting in. She was weary, and we had to leave, so as not to be out after dark when the countryside can become hazardous. It had been a long day.

We had arrived at the village early that day. Their landlord was already there. The Pastor simply gazed. Grief hung over us all for them for the loss of two precious members of their community. Under a bright clear blue sky and warm early Autumn day his sons sat with him, as well as the old men and young. All were dressed neatly in traditional *shalwar chemise*, the baggy pants and long collared shirt.

Their Muslim landlord had come to pay his respects to his tenant farmers coming to terms with the loss of one of their young men, as well as the Pastor's wife's sister. The landlord sat imperiously, larger in build, grander in dress with his white outfit and traditional Sindh hat. It is a simple disc for a crown and a narrow brim brightly jewelled, fitting his head closely. The golden glint of his cap could have been a crown, as he certainly ruled over this community as their landlord. They were his hardworking tenant farmers.

This was men's business only, so I joined the women in the shelter further down the slope. Here I found the mother and grandmother of the 19-yr. old young man who had suddenly died. The mother looked at me as I entered the shaded place for women. Gaunt weary eyes looked out from a blue *dupatta* head covering, plaintively asking. Her old mother sat close to her looking into the distant space without answer. How could they lose someone so precious to them? It was not a full week since he had taken suddenly ill and died within hours. Such is death in this place. It comes hungrily, giving no time for medical care or aid. The women of the community had come to sit with her.

I sat down close to the despairing mother. I perceived she might not have slept since her son's passing. She was exhausted. She easily without resistance let me nurse her as one would nurse a child. Her frame was light with sparse flesh. She let out small cries as I prayed and rocked her. She fell asleep in my arms. I lay her down on a quilt, placing her head on a pillow and wrapped her securely with her large dupatta as a swaddling. Even though the day was warm, there was little heat in her body. The grandmother looked at her daughter in concern. We both put our hands on her and prayed. These lovers of Jesus had someone taken too young. It was more than they could comprehend.

Sisters in the community called later to wail with her as is their loving custom. A plaintive guttural sound of lament sustained in rhythmic waves, resonated from the sunshade into the open field. The mother later woke and joined them.

My name was called. The landlord's condolence visit had ended, and he had departed. A memorial worship service was beginning. Women were included. Those women still grieving stayed behind in the shelter with their friends. Song broke out from the worship group gathering further up the rise, as young and old broke into hymns of praise. Only Jesus in their heart could bring such music.

The message of the death and resurrection of Christ, and the hope of the glory to come was spoken by our preacher and the pastor's son. This was not the end. Softly joyous worship was sung, and smiles spread from hearts that were being comforted.

11.

TELL THEM I'M ALIVE

Families came from a distant village for food supplies. They arrived in brightly painted wagons. The centre for distribution was a cluster of buildings with courtyards around a Hindu temple. Men and brothers, fathers and sons waited for their names to be called to go forward for the supplies given out. Weary and humbled, but with eagerness they strode across the courtyard into the small room set aside where bags of flour, oil and dried food were handed out. Each man came out with the bag hoisted on his shoulder with a smile of triumph. They had waited for this.

Outside the wall enclosing the temple was a courtyard where women traditionally sit, in the shade, unable to go into the temple inside. I was directed to this area. Our Pakistan Christian interpreter on the team sat with me for protection as a woman alone. It was also shelter from the intense heat. He and I sat chatting just waiting when we heard a soft, busy murmur. We could hear the sound of footsteps on dry clay getting nearer. A woman came through the gateway with open arms and smiling. She was eager to hug me. Others followed close behind with the same happy smile. They had seen us as they were arriving in their wagon.

I looked into the face of the one first to enter, and realized she was one of the women I had prayed for in the village where "Jesus" was whispered again and again. It was her embroidered quilt and cushions that had been brought out for me to lie down on, in shade from the heat. She had plugged in her fan to help me recover. It was a joyous hug this time. It was her hugging me. She sat closely as more came smiling in recognition, with open arms. They chatted to our interpreter in excitement at seeing us again. He was so captivated by seeing the women one by one greeting me and hugging me, he captured it on my camera.

We all moved to a shaded porch at the rear of the temple. I sat on the edge of the portico as they were sitting cross-legged on the ground. The chatter died down and we all sat looking and smiling at each other. My companion interpreter turned to me and said:

> *"I think they want you to say something. You speak, and I'll interpret."*

It was an unexpected opportunity. I quickly asked Jesus what to say. The words came to me:

> ...."*Tell them I'm Alive*".... "*Tell them that I love them*".

Instantly I recalled an experience 30 years ago, while sitting in my kitchen and reading God's Word. I had a disturbing awareness that someone out of view had entered the room and was standing there, behind me. I was afraid. I realised it was a person I couldn't see. I believed instantly it was the presence of Jesus. With eyes

closed but a clear picture in my awareness of Him, I flung myself
on the floor, at His feet and wept. I knew it was Jesus.

Through my tears but with eyes still closed, I could see a deep
furrow in each foot. It seemed He said: "*Get up!*" I got up. I looked
into His face. It shone with love. A love I had never known. I
looked into the palm of His left hand that He offered me. It too
had a deep furrow of a scar. I stroked His lower arm above his
hand. It seemed the very cells of His skin were composed of love.
A fire radiated from His forehead. His eyes spoke love.

In simple phrases and with each interpreted, I recounted that to
the women. I looked into their faces and said:

> *"Jesus died for you and for me". I used gesture to show
> His arms aloft and how nails had been driven into His
> hands, His feet. I told them what I was like, that my
> life was sad. I had thought and done things to make
> God sad and angry. That is how we all are. When Jesus
> was being killed all the wrong things I had done, all my
> sorrow, were paid for to satisfy God. Jesus didn't stay
> dead. He got up from the dead. He is alive, now! If we
> come to Him and say sorry, He will forgive us and give
> us new life. God can become our Father". "He knows
> you. He loves you...." I repeated: "Jesus loves you, He
> loves you...He is alive now and loves you!".*

In simple phrases and with each word carefully interpreted by
my companion at a gentle pace, I told them of that encounter with
Jesus in terms they could take in and comprehend. They listened
with attentive eyes. Our Pakistani interpreter then prayed for the
women in Urdu. He wept for them as he prayed. Culturally, the

experience of a Pakistani man weeping for them as women was a strange and wonderful gesture.

I marvelled that God had brought these women 65 kilometres from our first encounter where they received a Jesus hug, and echoed His name many times over. Now they had heard in their own language who He is, and what He has done for us.

As I was speaking to the women under the portico, inside the temple our Ethiopian preacher brother was shown a grave. He had it explained to him that it held the body of a dead ancestor whom they revered. He responded by telling the men that we too worship someone who had died, but who had not stayed dead. He had risen from the grave. Our preacher was given freedom to teach the Word of God and salvation through the death and resurrection of Christ. He told the men listening that new life was available to them if they believed.

That day as our preacher taught in the temple, one man of importance in this central village gave his life to Christ. We came on another day and held a worship and teaching time in a small room on this new believer's farm. The room had once been a Hindu place of worship, but now a place of worship and learning about Jesus.

12.

FESTIVAL OF EID

For three days in November the Muslims celebrate as they believe, Abraham's son Ishmael being saved from being sacrificed and a ram provided in his place. They celebrate it by killing a beast, carving it and sharing it, and inviting their friends to a feast. On one of our flood relief trips, we passed a livestock sale, in full swing. Hundreds were gathered to purchase their beast, for celebrating the Festival of Eid.

Come the day for slaughter, while walking to the local corner shop back in Rahim Yar Khan, I noticed men in the park up ahead, leaning over a bloodied carcass. I realized it was a cow that had been killed for Eid. Blood flowed out onto the grass. Later I looked down the adjacent street and a rickshaw cart was being loaded with another carcass. I saw the same slaughter again in the park near the shopping centre and again down a street walking home. I could smell the warm blood which had been spilt in and around our streets.

For the first night of Eid there is celebration everywhere. While standing in the centre of the city with a friend, the men, women and children were out in festive mood. It compared to our New Year's Eve in its atmosphere. Every possible light was turned on festooning the shop windows and bazaar stalls. "Salaam!" was called from passers-by. Even the eager rickshaw driver looking for a passenger when we refused, nodded very respectfully with a "Salaam!". The day before I had gone to share an Eid meal with a Muslim family on a very prosperous farm. It was an Eid meal with a difference.

For this Eid meal we set off very early. The morning promised a day of heat as we left Rahim Yar Khan to travel many kilometres into the Punjab countryside. We were on our way, first to a Christian brother's farm. The vast acres of fields were speckled with white bolls of cotton. The colourful head-covering of the women picking cotton, moved at a distant pace. The sky was a warm blue as we arrived at the friend's property.

Our host brought couches out for the men to sit in the open and talk. Our preacher-teacher and the men opened the Scriptures together. This was an interlude before we were to set off for his Muslim neighbour's farm further in the distance. Our hostess made chai for everyone. While the men studied and talked, a friend of the family took me out into the nearby field, where one could see closely the red, the yellow, all coloured head-coverings of the cotton pickers moving slowly. By now, even at mid-morning the sun's intensity was palpable. Such was the heat the women worked in.

After refreshments and talk, we were off. Our host, a strong believer, had nurtured a long-term friendship with his Muslim neighbour, some kilometres away. The four-wheel truck moving off, was full of Urdu chatter and expectations of an Eid meal. It was by invitation from this friend, as well as his brothers and their children. We travelled through lush prosperous countryside, arriving late morning.

Custom dictates always that the women sit apart when discussions are held between men.

This day was no exception. The men sat on couches under a pleasant portico. I was ushered into the cottage room adjacent in the courtyard. It was cooler inside, but the room was crowded. It was a gathering of around twenty family members. Women of several generations with young husbands, brothers and children, were seated on double beds.

Some were standing to make way for me to take a place. A cover was laid on a single couch especially for me. I was invited to lie down, but I declined. I still felt uncertain. I was more comfortable sitting on the edge of the couch looking out at the gathering.

The faces looked at me intently. My lack of their language meant broken words of English or small phrases, helped along with gesture, were the means of our conversation. We looked at each other, and smiled and coo-ed over the small babe in one of the young women's arms. The proud father beamed a smile, and told me how many weeks-old the child was by the number of fingers he held up. The baby refused to settle so it was given to the great-grandmother to nurse. It fell asleep quickly in her arms.

A cool drink was brought for me, with further gestures for me to lie down.

"What is Eid?" I asked a young man who had walked into the room, and stood looking at me. He did not quite understand. I

repeated gently to another sitting close-by me. A young teenage boy interpreted for the older.

"What is Eid?" I wanted to be the student, rather than the teacher I was usually introduced as. The younger brother helped him reply in simple isolated English words that they celebrate Ishmael being saved from being sacrificed at Mt. Moriah, by his father Abraham.

They are happy that a ram was provided instead.

"Muslim?" the baby's father asked me.

"Christian" I answered. *"I love Jesus"* holding my hand on my heart, then my hands together meaning worship. He just looked at me. I held out my arms, as Jesus on the Cross, and enacted the nails being driven into His palms, and dropping my head. It was a crude effort. *"Jesus...sacrifice...dead"* I spoke. The young father frowned. The rest puzzled. The baby slept and the great-grand-mother smiled at me.

Unnoticed, a young man had slipped in and was sitting at the back of the family on a double couch. He had seen my gestures and understood my words. He looked stern. Was it hostility? Perhaps he was afraid. He brooded intensely over what I had just said, not shifting his dark gaze from me. I became weak in my body. It was hot in the room and I was needing to lie down.

The women spoke in quick agitated Urdu while a cover was brought for me. I closed my eyes and prayed as I lay there. I prayed for the Holy Spirit to come and help them. I had just brought a message utterly challenging their own belief. It was hard for them. I was a guest and in their genuine care and warmth, they let me sleep.

I felt them looking over me, chattering quietly to themselves. I could hear the murmur of their voices, and I asked Jesus to come and explain to them what I had just 'spoken' in gesture of His death and sacrifice. It was a restoring rest, though not a sleep. The crowded room became quiet. I heard most of them leave.

Food was brought for me, my portion of the Eid meal the men were eating under the portico. The young mother who had given her baby to the great-grandmother noticed my hair was needing tidying. The dupatta had shifted, and my hair was in disarray. She brought a comb and unclipping my own hairclips, gently and slowly combed my hair. It was such a gesture of care. She moved hurriedly to the back of the room, searching through boxes to find one of her own hairclips to hold a stray strand of hair in place. I still have that little clip. The day edged on in slow motion, until I was called to join the men in the portico for Bible Talk.

I was asked to move to the back of the gathering under the shelter, giving place to the head of the household, his brothers, and his sons. I sat with my arm around the great-grandmother who had joined me. She smiled at me, our sole communication. Our teacher gave a message in Urdu of "Sacrificing the Beloved Son", of Jesus dying on the Cross to satisfy the wrath of God, for our sin. He explained that Jesus was the Eid sacrifice. The men and the great-grandmother next to me listened intently. They heard of the new life offered to us who believe.

A call was made from the preacher, and a number responded with their right hand lifted in acknowledgement that they had heard the truth. A closing prayer in Urdu completed the day. Soft chatter and farewells began. It was time to leave. I caught the face of the young man who had so sternly and fearsomely looked at me in the cottage room when I had spoken in gesture of Jesus the Sacrifice. He now looked at me with a clear gaze and a most beautiful radiance. A transformation had occurred when listening to our preacher.

He now smiled at me with a new glow in his eyes. I saw the same beauty in his father.

For them it was a different Eid. Regular Bible teaching and worship services led by a local pastor is now held in his home with his sons.

13.

FATHER HEART OF GOD

The time came to leave Rahim Yar Khan for our organisation's annual conference in Lahore. All the workers gathered from all over Pakistan. I travelled North by coach the way I had come, but this time by night. It was a fitful rest as it is law that travelling at night the lights in the coach must be kept on. This is so everyone can be seen for security purposes. I occasionally enjoyed putting my face close to the window and cupping my hands around my eyes to look out at the sleeping townships. They were barely lit, with shops closed, and stalls put away. An occasional dog sniffed the dust. It was a nostalgic journey away from Rahim Yar Khan. I recalled not quite four weeks before coming in daylight with no knowledge whatsoever of what lay ahead. I was told that anyone who has been to Rahim Yar Khan, manages somehow to return, but for now Moses with his mobile was fast asleep.

The conference was a rich mix of fellowship with brothers and sisters scattered all over Pakistan, from a diverse range of contexts. We were led in teaching by a newly retired Pastor from a large church in South Korea. He taught on the Father Heart of God, and how the Father's love needs to be in and through all that we do. He spoke of the blessing but also, the responsibility of pastoring. He described the pain of criticism, and the contest from false brethren. His face was soft and mellow, as he came alongside us personally, and asked after us, as to how we were managing. The gracious patience that God had worked into his soul and manner was a ministry of its own. I still can hear his pleading voice to us to remember Whose children we are.

Some of the workers at this conference came from distant places. One of them was a Korean lady working in the Thar desert of the Sindh Province. She works with orphaned children, among poor and marginalized Hindus and Hindu-Muslims. There is a great need for qualified schoolteachers to work in their Genesis School. The temperatures can reach extremes in this region and I marvelled at her joy and resilience.

Two Ethiopian couples provided some exuberant worship times. Having been working for some years in Pakistan, they were both fluent in Urdu, and as well in English. Both men rose early in the morning in Rahim Yar Khan where they were based, and prayed in the church next to my unit. Both men are strong in the Word of God. I would hear their resonant voices in prayer, shouts of joy and then pleading with God for the church and the people of Pakistan. It is a memory then and now which still inspires me. Both are men of fervent prayer, as are their wives, women of intercession.

When the Conference closed I made the coach trip from Lahore, further north to the capital of Islamabad where I was to teach English.

14.

SCHOOL IN THE CITY

Strange, dull, murky light hung over the city of Islamabad, an ordered, planned city with tall high-rise apartments and office blocks. Arterial roads run in all direction, busy with the cars that the prosperous own. They live in grand houses with their large extended families.

It is Pakistan culture, rich or poor, for the sons once married, to live with their parents and raise their family. The wealthy build grand multi-storey homes to accommodate them. The not so prosperous live in high-rise dwellings, or more modest homes in Rawalpindi.

There are many poor in Islamabad. You see them in the regional bazaars. They sit on the side of the busy main thoroughfare, cloaked in brown shawls, hugging warmth at nightfall by tins of refuse gathered in the street and set alight. Some cook a humble meal over the flames. Many do not survive the bleak winter.

The smell of drains lingers in the air, along with gas and car fumes. The presence of security seems everywhere. Private homes have an armed guard. Security police check your bag and scan you for dangerous weapons before allowing you to go into a collective group. The English For Life School where I had come to teach, had this constant watch and was under strict coaching from the secret police. Each of the 200 students was checked daily as they came into the school. The students liked it that way as it made them feel secure.

The English For Life School was set up for teaching English to Afghan Refugees in Islamabad. In former years the students were refugees from the Russian invasion, but at this time, they had fled the Taliban insurgents in their country. Afghans are merely tolerated in Pakistan. They are kept safe by vigilance. The school is a constant concern of the police. Staff are coached regularly for the students' and their own safety.

It is a very ordered School for English, following the Oxford Syllabus from Elementary to Advanced levels. Students must pass exams to be given a Certificate at each level.

Competency in English, both written and spoken is an asset for entry into university and employment. It gives social confidence and dignity to those who have been displaced from their homeland because of conflict. Some return to Afghanistan better equipped, others have moved overseas, but there is a huge population of Afghan refugees still in Islamabad.

Many have gained worthwhile employment. Others have found it very difficult. My classes were composed of women, 11 in all, who were needing extra tutoring with their English. Some of these women were beginner students. They had been staying at home, without opportunity to learn or socialize, having raised a family while coping with displacement.

I also taught two young men first thing in the morning before they went off to work. Both had a high level of competency. Both were needing more opportunity to express their English. We had some valuable conversations, by which I was richly informed. One had come as an infant in his mother's arms from Afghanistan, the other as a young child. The latter remembered, when very young, living in Afghanistan, being very sick in the night.

His mother lifted the curtain to check whether it was safe enough to take him to the doctor. As she lifted the muslin, he saw through the window, the explosion from the Russian rocket attacks lighting up the night sky and his mother deciding it wasn't safe to go. They later escaped across the border to Pakistan.

All the students enriched me with sharing their lives in some small way. One of my students was a principal of an Afghan primary school in Islamabad. Her response was eager and progressive in the eternal sense, a delightful woman who affectionately and gratefully gave me a gift of a lovely necklace. There was great rejoicing over her.

Before each lesson I would pray asking God to help me and help them. I asked for His presence to be there with us. On one occasion a student asked me *"How do you know God so well?"* I loved the simplicity of the question.

Because I was asked to explain my relationship with Father God, that is exactly what I did, telling them my testimony of God's saving grace in Jesus. One student one morning, after I had prayed, threw up her hands and said:

"Oh...I believe!". It would seem she had a revelation of our Father's reality in Christ by means of the Holy Spirit. It was a moment of triumph.

Some of my students allowed me to pray with them for their personal needs. Many carry deep scars of the soul. The separation from loved ones is always there for them They are strangers in a land, but not able to return home. I was free to return to my home in Australia. They're not free to do that easily or with any sense of long-term stability.

After some weeks, in a climate of constant surveillance and continual attention to politically appropriate words and actions, I began to feel the strain. One morning on entering another teacher's class I knocked strongly and rapidly on the door. My hands were cold in the winter's morning and I suddenly lost my grip on the door handle. The handle hit the door with a violent bang. The door flew open hitting the wall of the room. A male student in the classroom broke down. He thought the sudden door opening and the loud click of the handle, a gunshot. He sobbed with his head on the desk. I was so saddened that my swift action had caused him that pain. Such are the embedded memories of war.

I had come to the School after teaching young students in Rahim Yar Khan, and going out every opportunity with the flood relief team. Over one period of 10 days I had sat and comforted as many people, both in the flood zone, but also in Rahim Yar Khan city. It began to impact my strength. Under the oppression of Islamabad it was compounded. I came to tears, longing for the familiar, the faces of my family and friends. It is called culture shock fatigue and my discerning supervisor carefully suggested it was time to go home. It came as a surprise as I had every intention of staying longer in Islamabad. She spoke affirming, loving words. She assured me a task had been completed well.

I sensed it was right to go home, but not until going to Quetta 600 kms west of Islamabad.

It is the capital of Baluchistan province on the border with Afghanistan.

I did not want to go home before at least seeing the place where the Hazara Afghans live as refugees, on the boundary of this city. I knew from my research and conversations in my homeland, that the Hazara Afghans are treated with scorn. But there was another good reason for going to Quetta. At our organisation's conference I had met up with a Japanese missionary who worked in the Christian Hospital there. Kumiko begged me to come to see if I could help the Autistic children and their mothers, who came to the hospital. No large-scale facility existed for these children.

While I certainly was not experienced in this specific field, as a speech therapist I was familiar with cognitive disorders in language and speech. I agreed to go and see what help I could facilitate. It was an official invitation from the Medical Director of the Christian Hospital that I based the legitimacy of my entering Quetta. No proof was asked for, but I had it with me, in case. Entry can be refused as it is considered a dangerous city.

My plane ticket was booked for me and I flew out two days later, for the city in the mountains. Even though the security was tight in that city, I was so happy to at last be going to where my prayers had initially centred, on the Hazara Afghan people. If I could also bring some assistance for the Autistic children and their mothers, it would be a bonus.

Sadly, the English for Life School that I was leaving, would be closed two months later.

Militants sent a note, threatening slaughter. Packing and removal of resources was done swiftly and painfully. It was the closure of many years of faithful servants' work for displaced and hurting refugees.

15.

GOD IS OLD

I looked out of the window. Two young Pakistani men, mining engineers, enthusiastically had moved to give me the window seat for our flight from Islamabad to Quetta. I was a guest in their country. Instilled in the Pakistan conscience is the rule always to honour a guest. For this trip I was theirs.

For the 1 ½ hour flight the plane flew at comparatively low altitude across the entire breadth of Pakistan south-westwards, towards the border with Afghanistan. Out of my window I could see the 12,500 feet peaks and crags of the Suleiman Range with occasional green. The green appeared from this height as pockets of moss, providing fodder for clusters of farmland livestock. They were grazing on steep slopes. The villages were closeted into the ravines, small clusters of life here and there, sheltered under mighty peaks.

"God is ancient" I said, pointing heavenward.

"Ancient?" the one who spoke English puzzled. He did not know the word.

"Old....God is old" I said, pointing heavenward again.

"Yes, yes..." He nodded in agreement and wonder, leaning over to see out the window with me.

Did we acknowledge the same God? I couldn't answer that. The landform below us looked ancient and I pondered the Hand that had formed it. That same Hand is the one I trust for my shelter and my clothing, for my very well-being. These infinitely small concerns were important to Him who is our trusted heavenly Father. The God who had created these forbidding mountains from old, had adopted me as His child.

My eyes misted when I looked down on tiny clusters of villages, cradled within the grand peaks and registered that our Father loved the people who lived in those homes, and farmed the land. He loved them with the same love with which He loves me. I prayed that that same grace in Jesus that enabled me to be His adopted child, would be known by them. We flew over many of these sheltering villages.

The plane momentarily shuddered, and the engine swelled in intensity, but our plane was not going forward. It started shaking, then shaking more strongly. We were suspended over these mighty peaks, hovering. The engines were brought back to less intensity, as if waiting, idling, shaking.

"I hope it isn't going to stop here!" I begged the young man next to me. He chuckled and said:

"Happens always to Quetta, same place." He explained the draughts created by the massive mountain peaks, compete and hold the plane in this space. I was reassured, waiting. The space

of waiting seemed very long to me. Suddenly the plane gained power and surged forward, gathering momentum, flying out over the clear plains.

"You now in Quetta" my companion assured me, with a smile.

The exit doors of the airport in Quetta opened to a clear blue sky. A rifle was aimed directly towards me. My heart leapt. In peace I looked longer into the face of the one who was aiming. His black eyes were focused on the exit door, brooding in concentration under his military camouflage hat. His rifle was aloft his shoulder, finger on the trigger, ready. I walked out of his range. He maintained his prepared stance aiming at the exiting passengers. Some security alert must have been warranted. Others like him were in herringbone arrangement in the clear space outside the airport.

They were on duty. Quetta is a military headquarters close to the border of Afghanistan.

Security is tight and on permanent alert. It is comparatively clean and orderly as a regional city, 5,500 feet above sea level, within the 10,000 feet Takatu Mountains.

My first delight in Quetta was Kumiko, who met me at the airport. For these five days she was intent on taking me wherever I wanted to go, intent on blessing me. She even went to the trouble of shopping for pomegranates and lovingly and patiently ground the seeds in a mortar and pestle. The drink was delicious.

Kumiko nurses in the Christian Hospital situated in a busy thoroughfare of the city. It is a testament to God's keeping power that she has been kept through repeated seasons of dangerous unrest in the 27 years she has been in Pakistan, 10 of them in Quetta.

As an only child in Japan, her father passed away when she was 2 years old. She was led to Christ when she was in her teens by a Baptist missionary. Her mother later became a Christian and has faithfully supported her through all this time.

After training as a nurse, she went to Bible College then entered Missionary training. She took me through her photo album of these preparatory years and the different places in Pakistan where she has worked, including the early days of working in the refugee camps.

I wondered if all those years ago, the missionary to Japan ever imagined that the teenager she led to Christ would become such a soldier for Him, one with such a pearly face as hers. Kumiko is greatly loved and appreciated by Muslims and Christians for her presence in the hospital. She has a skill with difficult dressings and is called on in emergencies to assist the less experienced. This she does willingly as well as her normal shifts. At each period of political instability when it has been suggested to her to come home, she has said *"Why?"* Such is her enduring commitment.

Kumiko knew my particular interest was the Afghan Hazara people, so she took me to the suburb of Mehra Bad which houses the Hazara Pakistanis from the 1930's and thereafter the late 70's and 80's. When the Russians invaded Afghanistan, they came over the border in thousands. They are called Hazara Pakistanis, established citizens in this border city, where second and third generations now live. There is a quiet earnest vigour in their town.

Businesses happily opened to the early winter sun. Smiling shopkeepers, happy to be photographed, stood with their wares. Young men walked confidently. They showed little hesitancy at my asking could I take a photograph, and posed with pride, older and young, all men. With the occasional exception, women were seldom seen, during this season of Muhurrum. Some children were in the streets but not many. Two little girls hooded in black let me take their photo.

The season of Muharram is when Shi-ites mourn the death of the Cousin of Mohammed. For this season, they process in the street, shrouded in gruesome black and chant, holding flags. As Kumiko was driving up a narrow street, a group of them came by surprise around a corner, heading straight towards our small Suzuki. Kumiko was afraid and we prayed for protection as they moved closer to our jeep and surrounded it either side, shouting vehemently, but then passed on. We were relieved. It is a morbid chant, a protesting, begging wail. Another group appeared but we were prepared and able to move away.

I admired the sunny street with stalls and shops being opened on a late Monday morning, with business as usual. I got out of the jeep to capture it on camera. Some called to their friends to be included in the shot. Repeats were requested as they wanted someone else in the photo. A man in a brown blanket squinted in the sun for the camera and smiled.

I said:

"*Thank you*" and returned to the jeep, but it wouldn't start for Kumiko. Every effort to kick over the engine failed. What would we do? A man noticed we were in trouble and came to offer to push, while my hostess turned the ignition key, but to no avail. The vehicle just wouldn't start. I got out of the jeep but was rebuked as a woman. It was for men to do, not a woman. I stood aside. The jeep was pushed into a street strategically chosen, while one of the young men walked briskly to an auto-mechanic up a laneway. It was salvation with a bonus.

The mature Hazara mechanic warmed eagerly to Kumiko, as he explained he had friends from Japan. He lifted the bonnet and looked. No reason except for 'no petrol'. Someone was sent to get the petrol. It was an interval worth having, waiting. An elderly man came out of his shop to the chatter and activity outside.

He smiled and said to me:

"*Where from?*"

"*Australia...*"

"*Australia*" he echoed with a warm smile, nodding. "*Visitor?*"

"*Visitor*" I nodded. "*English teacher. I teach English*". Grinning, he told me he also had been a teacher, of Engineering Draughting.

"*I now am a bookbinder*" He looked very happy to be that. A friend joined us. I captured them on camera. It was a delightful exchange. Their welcome was genuine.

The petrol came, and we were off. It was time to go home. Driving towards the large circular intersection at the entrance to Mehra Bad, a man waved us to stop and asked me not to take photos. He must have seen me further back and recognized our vehicle. We had come to a chilling place. In the same large intersection, 60 Hazaras, Shi-ites, were murdered by a Sunni suicide bomber less than 3 months before. They were simply watching a procession. There was still a lingering death over the intersection. Kumiko became afraid. The caution to put my camera away had come as a reminder that this place of slaughter was still deeply sensitive for the residents.

"*This is where Hazaras killed. September*". Kumiko spoke fearfully, furtively, her eyes flashing to every point of the intersection, not trusting that sinister plans might not again be carried out.

"*Carnage. Terrible carnage*" she spoke with fresh fear.

The heavy military presence in the spherical intersection promised distrust. It was Muhurram and Hazara Shi-ites are despised targets of the Sunnis in practicing their season of mourning. It was a time of alert for everyone, military, police and civilians.

A brooding belief that all was not well.

16.

CHRISTIAN HOSPITAL

On the day after arriving in Quetta, as arranged by Kumiko and the Medical Director of the Christian Hospital, I came to talk with parents of Autistic children. They, with their children were in the Resource Centre on this crisp cold Saturday morning. The Centre consists of one room made available to them for a daily playgroup. It was arranged in small activity areas, very lightly equipped with toys and learning tools. They were asking for help.

While as a speech therapist I have worked with children with language and speech disorders, Autism is a specialist field in which I have not worked. With no other worker for support, it seemed that with the knowledge I do have, I could help them gather information and access resources. It was a morning of observing the children and listening to the parents.

In Quetta and beyond, Autistic children or children with any disability are hidden from view.

It is considered a shame to have a child with any disability. No exact figure could be given to me that morning, but it is estimated in the Quetta region there would be hundreds of children with Autism, or related disabilities who have never been seen, but are sheltered within the four walls of their home. Mothers with a disabled child do not emerge out of shame. They are hidden.

One of the children I saw that morning, a son, adopted at 2 weeks old, proved to be severely disabled. It was his adoptive mother who had worked so hard to establish this simple Resource Centre. She was a trained teacher within a normal school setting. It was her compassionate vision for Christ's love to be ministered to those hidden children and their mothers that stirred my will to endeavour to help. She hoped first, to enrol in a 12- month Autistic Teacher Training Course in Karachi. Her commitment to help them proved a deep challenge for her. I intended to invest the following year in endeavouring to raise funds to help her. On returning home, a small cluster of women in my church family shared my hope. Funds were raised for her to do the Teaching Course so she set off for Karachi. It was a start.

Having seen the plight of these children, my hope was to assist in the establishment of a facility to help them and their mothers. I was yet to learn that while my heart and other's hearts are fully committed to bringing life to these needy children, politics and individual intentions can be difficult to navigate.

17.

HAZARA TOWN

A final and resolving joy was to visit the place called Hazara town. It is the town of the Hazara Afghans more recently come to Pakistan. They are refugees from the tyranny of the Taliban in their homeland. It was originally to them that I was asked by our organisation, would I go? When I responded and applied, the situation in Quetta had become too unstable. Default plans were put in place. Now Kumiko and I were to visit.

Before we set off from Quetta city, we were met by a young man Joya. He was to accompany us to where he lived with his family in this new refugee settlement under the forbidding mountains 125 kilometres from the border with Afghanistan.

After leaving the city we drove some kilometres across a dusty pink plain. The air was crisp as we passed newish buildings, stalls and every sign of busy trade wherever crowds were gathered. Donkeys pulled loads of goods and people. Smaller trucks were loaded with wares and an occasional motor bike passed us as we approached the newly built overpass. It was a gentle ascent, with at first, peaks of mountain in sight. As our small four-wheel drive made its way to the crest of the overpass, the mountains and the homes came into full 180 degrees view.

It instantly evoked the image that may have been of the children of Israel camped under Mt. Sinai. Here in a sweeping canvas, stretching for kilometres, were small houses still in the dusty pink of newness sheltering under a mountainous backdrop from which they were hewn. Jesus' words came to my mind: "*A field white to harvest*", meaning that there were many in this town of refugees whose heart would be soft to hearing about Him. The Hazara Afghans are a people who are not wanted by the Pashtun Afghans in their own land, but even less so in Pakistan as refugees.

Joya lived with his father and mother in a soundly built home in a busy thoroughfare of the town. Eleven years before when the Taliban had threatened their village, the family escaped from the hills of Ghazni province in Afghanistan. Joya was thirteen years old when they left their goat farm and travelled by treacherous roads through the mountainous border to Quetta. As they travelled by these dangerous roads Joya was given the task of hiding under his legs a huge bag of Afghan coins, their mother and father's hard-earned savings.

Having had his education disrupted in these years he had returned to school and now was studying for his Matriculation. He had hopes of entering university. To support his family, he was working in the afternoons, after attending school in the morning. Joya's older brother had been a valuable, highly skilled interpreter working with the U.S Army in southern Afghanistan when he was killed out on patrol. The grief of his death still lingered for them as they opened their gate to welcome us.

We were invited into a front room especially laid with fine mattresses to sit on richly embroidered cushions. Green tea was served with sweet foods. Kumiko was a treasured guest to their home. She had some years earlier, nursed Joya's older sister when she was seriously ill in the Christian Hospital. At that time little hope was held for her survival, but under Kumiko's loving care as well as the family's constant vigilance, Joya's sister recovered. I was now greeted as a family friend, simply by being a friend of Kumiko.

With extended family joining us, our hours of chatting and eating with them, were closed with Kumiko praying. I couldn't have imagined a better finale to my time in Pakistan than this day. There was a calm sweet presence being together. It was my last day in this border city of Quetta. Flying north-eastward, the next morning, back over the Sulamain Range, this time the draughts created by the mountainous peaks assisted us. The journey back to Islamabad took 15 minutes less.

Being the 9th and 10th day of Muharrum for my last two days in Islamabad, we were all confined to our homes above the English School. The School itself was closed, as was the Girls' School over the road which usually hummed. No one could be seen in the street.

For the Shi-ites and the general public, these two final days of mourning, are the days of greatest risk. There are only two flights a week out of Islamabad to Bangkok. I was assured the hazard had passed by the evening of the 10th day when I would fly out.

With help I unloaded excess items from my luggage to bring down the weight and was trying to get the zipper shut when the taxi came. With help I scrambled into the taxi.

Looking back I saw the "*chowkidar*" (doorkeeper) standing in the driveway waving.

As a safeguard, whenever going out by myself I would tell him where and for what purpose. Now I was going home. He was still standing, waving., The empty streets meant the taxi made swift passage to the airport. I was on my way home.

PART 2
2011

18.

AUTISTIC CHILDREN

On returning to Australia, it was my aim to explore in the new year, all possibilities to help long-term the Autistic children in the city of Quetta. Every opportunity to share this need was taken. I heard with optimism, that our Australian government was willing to give hope and financial assistance through Foreign Aid to Women and Children of Pakistan.

This comprised Education and Health programmes assistance. I immediately made enquiries and was given the protocol to follow to explore the possibility of assistance.

Women friends at home met over these months, to pray for the Autistic children and their mothers. I researched thoroughly what would constitute the features of a valuable, medical and educational facility for the Autistic children, within the Christian Hospital. It absorbed months of contacting, relating and planning with experts in the field.

Because this was not my area of expertise, I hoped to facilitate others' knowledge and skills to see it become a reality. My hopes were geared to persevering in this. Having related over some months to the Foreign Aid Department in our own capital city, I then was connected to their department in the Australian Embassy in Islamabad. I was assured from both offices that the Autistic Clinic envisaged met all the criteria for financial assistance. It was not a huge amount of money in our western currency, but in Pakistan, resources and labour are very much less than ours. It would come in increments over 3 years. It was a subsidy to which the Christian Hospital was to provide an initial percentage of the overall cost for building to begin. My hopes were high. It would be the first of its kind in Pakistan, and the most comprehensive approach to meeting the needs of Autistic children.

I shared with our organisation in my homeland what I had researched regarding the Australian Aid Grant, and the idea of helping the Christian Hospital establish a clinic for the Autistic children. I was given the go-ahead to take this project to the Medical Director in Quetta. Armed with this knowledge and hope along with all necessary documentation I set off again for Pakistan. It was 12 months since my first timid entry into the unknown. My faithful church family contributed generously to enable me to make this second trip just as they had done for my first.

I was asked by our organisation if I would take with me a young woman who wanted to explore the possibility of working in such a context, given the religious and cultural restraints. She would prove to be a valuable companion in researching the multiple needs of children facing challenges in learning in this remote and dangerous city.

Our initial task was to research thoroughly and prove to the Australian Aid Office, that a substantial need existed for a Diagnostic and Development Centre for the children.

On arrival in Quetta we settled into a comfy cottage in the Christian Hospital staff residential area. The homes were set amidst an English garden with the loveliest trees.

Sadly, the city outside the gates was far from settled. Violence was occurring on a regular basis.

It was wonderful to be back with Kumiko, our Japanese missionary nurse whose faithful face met us at the airport. It was different from my last journey to, and arrival in Quetta. There was no turbulence this time flying further south over the lower range of the Sulamain peaks from Lahore. No guns were levelled at us as we came through the exit gate. Sun shone, and families welcomed their travellers. It was a replacement of grim memories of the last year during the season of Muhurram. Pakistan is a place of contradictions and the unexpected.

We wasted no time in talking in various rounds with executive staff of the Hospital. It was a delicate process observing cultural boundaries and another cup of tea or coffee for every round of discussion. It took great concentration remembering names, including my own, as only a while before, I was shopping in my local shopping centre back home.

I begged the Lord for mercy in sustaining me in what promised to be a challenging process in introducing the possibility of establishing a Centre for the Diagnosis and Development of Autistic children.

I needed to explain in careful detail my suggestion of applying for an Australian Aid Grant to assist in the process of building an Autistic Centre. Later in the evening we had further discussion with a couple who were among the prime movers in this venture. They are parents of an Autistic son. They both loved Jesus and trusted Him, that something could be established for their son and others like him. We closed our time together in prayer to Father God for mercy.

Strong encouragement came for us with the commitment by the Medical Director, of a location within the Hospital for the Autistic Centre. All this depended on the assistance with the funding, and approval from the Hospital Directors to seek contributions from other sources. I sent a news update to my church family back home, asking them to pray. Plans were being drawn for the space within the hospital, for the envisaged centre.

The Architectural Draftsman and Contract Builder employed by the hospital worked out how to transform an unused ward and open area at the side of the Hospital. It was ideal.

The disused ward was verandah-styled, and up to now, full of junk and old beds, but soon to be cleared out and restored. It would be opened out with folding doors onto a play area designed especially for Autistic children.

It would be a Sensory Motor Playground to develop their skills. It would be safely encompassed within the Hospital, but with its own entrance gate. It would be called the Autistic Diagnostic & Development Centre, aiming to provide space for multi-disciplinary care. A room was designed for visiting consultants as well as a large room for every day teaching. Elsewhere in Pakistan each discipline is addressed in separate locations, not in one Centre. This would be the first.

My companion took charge of the research with carefully prepared questionnaires for teachers in the schools and medical staff when visiting the main hospitals. Each day brought a new task and a new situation. We were given a warm and helpful welcome wherever we went. Worthwhile conversations with principals and teachers revealed a tremendous gap in provision for diagnosis and development for children with Autism.

Discussions with the Medical Director of the Children's Hospital and Consulting Paediatrician came as confirmation from them, we were pursuing a worthwhile course.

Baluchistan is a forgotten province they all say, where highly skilled health professionals are at a premium. I believed only God could break through this lack. Unrest continually discourages workers coming from the major cities, perpetuating the frustration of those in Quetta who cannot possibly meet the overwhelming health and educational needs of children.

Each day we prayed for peace over the city. It was comparatively quiet for some days until the Head of the Pakistan Medical Association was target-shot dead. It was a loss of a mature and highly experienced Orthopaedic Surgeon. Such evil prevails against people of integrity. A deep lament came for such a one as he was.

I so appreciated my companion's company. She was refreshingly Aussie in her style, and gave the light touch to my more sober moments. At times we had to navigate the difference in our ages. I tried to understand what she must be seeing in me, an older lady with a bagful of medication, with a slower pace of processing thoughts as well as change of plans. She wore her Pakistan dupatta head covering with such style. Walking along together we could be mistaken for a movie star and the Old Woman Who Lived in a Shoe.

Seriously, she was a godly young woman, adjusting to the cultural strangeness but drawn to the people and the charm of the street stalls and bewildering traffic.

We needed to make allowances for each other, and not to quench the Spirit of the Lord who enabled us to listen to each other. My clumsy words on one occasion needed her forbearance, and on another, my lack of sensitivity to her, needed her forgiveness. In one instance of alarm in me when I heard in the dark, someone up the side of our house, she expressed a fiesty courage to confront them. It was simply a man on our roof cutting off trailing branches from next door's fence, strangely in the dark. It was probably one of the security men making our residence safer from someone climbing the fence via the trailing branches. I was glad I had her companionship.

In the daytime the beautiful setting of a garden with rich birdlife and leafy orchard next to our cottage, so helped one's morale. The weather was superb in this northern Autumn with clear blue skies.

On our very first school visit to research the needs of the children, a young boy was brought to me as one who had made no attempt to communicate or respond in classroom activities since being enrolled. His face and posture was sorrowful and his voice silent.

The principal explained this child was one of many children who come in from remote towns in the countryside. These tribal groups often follow very rigid cultural religious rules such as Purdah. This is the practice of the woman wearing a completely black head and body covering with only one eye showing. The children never see their mother's full face. I saw many in the shopping centre of Quetta. It is a very sinister outfit, inducing fear even for an adult looking on. How much more for a child who longs to see their mother's face. The principal said these children are often sent into the city to live with relatives and she believes some are not treated kindly, but in fact are abused. Such factors she considered, caused this boy's muteness and lack of participation.

I asked if I could pray for him. The teacher agreed, and I gently laid my hand on his head, smiling and speaking softly. I prayed for Jesus to touch this child's heart and mind and soul, releasing him from fear. As we were leaving the classroom, I looked back and he broke into a beautiful smile. It served as a deep encouragement to me. Jesus had broken the power of terror in him.

As a small interlude one evening we were invited to a missionary couple's home for dinner. An array of tasty dishes was prepared by their Kashmiri cook. It was refreshing to meet other workers in Quetta. Some were working with the Red Cross and others with Doctors Without Borders. Mingling and chatting was valuable, listening to their various projects of weight in this context.

I was already familiar with the work of the Red Cross. They had established an Amputee Clinic in the grounds of the Hospital. I had been shown this on my earlier trip to Quetta.

Each morning a substantial queue of patients waited for the clinic to open. Many have lost limbs in this province and essential prostheses are fitted for arms and legs. So frequent are bomb blasts that the clinic provides an essential on-going service.

A member of the Doctors Without Borders, on discovering I was a speech therapist asked me would I please go with them to an outlying village where they were working. They were given a young boy to examine. He was completely mute. They screen tested his hearing which appeared sufficient for speech. The Mental Health nurse believed he showed signs of having been traumatised like many children suffering from the ever-frequent violence they had witnessed. Given a break in the Autistic Centre project, I endeavoured to contact the team. Sadly, by then they were out of phone range and my willingness to go was frustrated. It was however, an indication that there were many needs of children in this troubled province.

After enjoying our meal, around the dinner table that evening, we retired to the loungeroom for coffee. The conversation was relaxed and the atmosphere mellow, when the floor shuddered and windows vibrated violently. Conversation stopped. A suicide bomb. We later learned it was 3 kms away at the Quetta Railway Station, The other guests seemed little disturbed and conversation resumed. For us, it was our first experience.

Some weeks later, over a meal with the Director of Nursing at the Hospital, one of his sons recounted to me, that he was driving home from work, a few weeks before, when the air shattered into a dark cloud of a bomb blast. Bodies lay in pieces around him. His shoulder was bloodied. He was disorientated, but still conscious. He explained to me that out of the clouds of dark dust, a man on a bike had come alongside the car and lifted him out and placed him on his push bike. The man walked, with him on his bike, to the nearest hospital and saw to it that he was laid on a stretcher and attended to. The son told me:

"I looked up to thank him, but he was gone. I believe it was an angel. How could a person appear so swiftly out of dark smoke and dust of such destruction, when nowhere at all could anyone or anything else be seen?"

After medical care the young man was healed in time for his planned marriage just a fortnight later. He told me: "It is a miracle. I was rescued, I was healed". He pulled back his shirt and showed me the minimal scar where a fragment of metal had gone right through his shoulder. Many died that day.

19.

ALONE

After three weeks of our daily trips to schools and hospitals, my companion had to leave Quetta and return to Lahore, as her visa was for a limited season. She needed to apply for an extension. In the meantime, her passport was withheld. It involved her making tedious repeated trips from Lahore to Islamabad to the government office who continued for the next 5 weeks to retain her passport. Her extension for her remaining month in Pakistan was finally granted. Poor phone reception meant I failed in my repeated attempts to keep in touch with her.

She later told me she had suffered a debilitating fever, while all alone in our organisation's unit in Lahore. Her days of fever were anguished with having to listen to livestock being slaughtered for Eid in the paddock next door. The smell of blood is sickening. Her description of the sickness was identical to what I had suffered some weeks earlier. It corresponded with the symptoms of Denghi Fever. We already knew there was an epidemic. It left us weakened.

I had had the benefit of robust anti-biotics and Kumiko nursing me back to strength with her carefully prepared chicken soup and refreshing fluids to drink. One of the doctors from the hospital came to check in on me and was shocked at my gauntness. She ordered me to rest, which I did. My companion in Lahore had none of this personal care which saddened me.

I was now in Quetta without her. I really missed her company, particularly in the cottage alone at night. While there were security men who regularly took walks at intervals around the house outside, my ears were vigilant for any unwarranted visitor. When I couldn't sleep easily I would sit outside and was kept assured by conversation with one of the officers on night duty. We sat and chatted in the courtyard by my backdoor. When finally settling back in my bed I would count the ever-present rounds of gunfire in the streets to go to sleep as one would count sheep. One night I counted 19 and before I could add the next round of 4 shots, I fell asleep.

Because the Army Headquarters were less than a kilometre away, and our cottage not far from the main road and major intersection, I knew when it was midnight. The army trucks rolled past with such nightly precision. One night when the aloneness overwhelmed me, I shut myself in the storeroom. I felt for one brief moment like a frightened child. I sat there until the midnight army trucks passed and the streets became quiet and went to bed.

These sinister sounds at night were replaced in the morning by a schoolgirl in the schoolyard over the fence, singing the morning chant to Allah. I didn't know the words of her song in Arabic, but her voice was perfectly clear and bell-like. It was the most exquisite music for the early morning. When I told the elderly gatekeeper of our hospital compound, how much I loved this singing, he hastily pointed to his chest, indicating it was his daughter.

He was old and had many children from his three wives each from a different generation.

On my previous visit to Quetta I had taken a collection of photos of his children who played around the residential cottages. I had the snapshots developed and gathered into an album. I asked him could I please come to visit him and his family? They lived in simple mud cottages at the back of the compound. I wanted to give them the gift of the album.

Sitting on a clay floor I was offered with enthusiasm green tea and sweet food. His wives huddled around the album, giggling in delight. The children jumped around them looking over their shoulder. The doorkeeper was very proud of his three wives and many children. The mothers allowed me to pray for them and their little ones.

There was still much to do to see the Autistic children's project we had worked on, continue. Meetings with the Medical Director and those on the Hospital Board were regular. In one distinct meeting with them as well as the Contract Builder, there was a blackout. We were all in sudden darkness. I could see nobody, but the voices continued as if nothing untoward had happened. I was amused and couldn't help chuckling at the continued earnest discussion between them. For them it was a regular occurrence, so business as usual, in the dark.

I continued to give God thanks for what seemed very purposeful intentions by the executives in the Christian Hospital to follow through with the envisaged Autistic Centre. All the documents were gathered including our Research Findings and

Recommendations. One vital step remained, and that was to have the Bishop of the Diocese' approval. It was under his jurisdiction. The funds required for the Hospital to outlay initial building costs needed his signature for the Application documents to be completed for the Australian Aid Grant. It was my intention that when these documents were finalised, I would go and present them to the Australian Aid Office in Islamabad. The person in charge of this department, told me she was looking forward to us meeting and discussing the project. It seemed there was every chance they would be short-listed for financial assistance, chosen from hundreds of applicants. My time in Quetta was running out. Final approval had not been given. I had to continue to wait.

When I was told the Bishop of Karachi's son had a Ph.D. in Autism Education, and headed up the Disabilities Programs in the Diocese, I wanted to travel down to the city in the South. I wanted to relay to him and his father, the vision for the Quetta, Christian Hospital. I also wanted to understand more fully, how they were addressing the issue of diagnosis and development for these children in their city. Sadly, the organisation I was working under could not allow me to go alone. It was against policy. Such ventures had to be with another person. No suitable person was available, so I had to forego that plan. It may have made our plans easier to be facilitated.

We were very conscious that the need in the children was on God's heart. We also knew only in His time, and with His provision. I was hopeful that once established our Mission organisation and others would be able to provide voluntary staff in the various roles of teaching and medical aid to supplement any local staff available.

In the process of collecting all the remaining completed questionnaires distributed to the school principals, I was waiting in a school playground while my driver parked his car around another street. This was a security measure, one of many taken while in this city.

As I waited, a class of children processed out of one building on their way to another.

One boy broke rank and ran up to me greeting me in Urdu. His face shone. It took a second before I recognised him. He was the child I had prayed for who was non-communicative when we visited the first time. A little boy who then, wasn't talking, hanging his head, hunching his shoulders and full of fear, now stood tall with a beautiful smile to say hello to me. As he went, I threw him a kiss. He responded with the same, and waved, before running off to join his mates. *Thank You Jesus!*

As the weeks passed gentle Autumn became cold nights and mornings. It was a sharp contrast. Quetta is up at 5,500 feet altitude and the chill crispness of early winter could be felt. I could still enjoy the sunshine during the day and the birds didn't seem put off by the cold. They chorused enthusiastically. It was a beautiful time of the year before the bitter cold sets in. My update to my friends at home recorded:

"The Lord prevails in love and mercy with power"

I continued to be encouraged as to the project we were working on.

You will recall that one of the mothers with an Autistic child had been the instigator of the simple playroom for the children when I visited on my first trip to Quetta. With the assistance of funds she had now completed her course in Karachi in Teaching

Autistic Children. She returned enthusiastically with the hope of using these newly acquired skills.

She and her husband arranged to meet up with me. She was eager to learn from the Medical Director of the plans being laid for the Diagnostic & Development Centre. She was encouraged and freshly fuelled in her hope.

It was a happy meeting in the Director's home, of course over a cup of tea. I left for a while to let her and the Director speak further, and went outside to keep her two sons happy on the swings in the garden. While they were playing and enjoying the sunshine, several rounds of gunfire resonated close-by. The children played on as if nothing had happened. While it startled me, they seemed oblivious. I was saddened that this sound of violence was a part of their background noise, and something as common as the sound of traffic. Quetta is certainly a place of unrest, and calamity. The children of this city know nothing else.

One evening while sitting with my laptop in the front garden of the cottage, hoping to catch the wi-fi, the ground under my feet heaved and shuddered. A split-second explosion.

The Medical Director appeared through the front gate.

"Jinnabad…. bomb".

He had picked up the announcement on his radio. It was 5 kilometres away, but the strength of the jolt indicated it was a huge detonation. I read a day or so later, a 16-yr. old young man, a Christian, had been kidnapped from the Catholic Community in Jinnabad, by militants. He was delivered back to his community, with a suicide vest locked onto him. It was detonated remotely by them. Heroically and sacrificially he chose to stand in a wide-open stretch of land, a considered distance from homes. He alone lost his life.

Maria, the one just having completed her Autistic Teaching qualifications was eager for me to see the block of land, she and her husband owned out of the city. It was their intention to build a residential facility for school-aged Autistic children from remote rural villages.

We drove out to Jinnabad, the place of the bomb blast two weeks before. As we were making our way through the small laneways of this Catholic Community our vehicle was blocked by guests walking to a wedding.

According to custom, relatives and friends were on their way to attach gifts of money to the bridegroom's clothing. Slowly our vehicle edged its way through the pedestrian crowd and out into an open space where the young man was waiting. He was royally dressed with fine headgear and richly decorated clothes. One by one as the guests arrived, relatives attached currency to his jacket, so he goes to his wedding with his torso covered in money.

To signal that the bridegroom was ready to go to his bride a triumphant shot was fired from a robust Russian Kalashnakov rifle just metres from where I was standing. A pain sliced through my head. I held my hands over my ears until the agony died away. It wasn't until much later, on returning home, when tested, that I learnt that that one gunshot had taken all my high-frequency hearing. From that moment onwards, I would not be able to hear the voiceless consonants of speech without hearing aids on both ears. As a speech therapist I had spent many years listening for, and training children to listen for spoken soft high-frequency sounds. Now I needed help.

20.

WAITING

For now, the days of waiting for the final plans and costings for the envisaged Autistic Centre gave opportunity for strolls through the bazaar, with valuable conversations, learning about the people and their stories. On each occasion I was offered the traditional cup of tea and learnt to accept. Initial fear in them of a westerner, was overtaken by assurance when they realised I had come to Quetta in peace.

One morning I sat in a laneway on a chair sipping tea that had been brought to me with a dozen pairs of eyes just looking at me. The huge wheels of a donkey dray brushed my chair, just missing my toes. As often I found out their families are from Afghanistan and were happy when I told them I had Afghan friends in Australia. It was then full acceptance was realised and they relaxed.

In one small shop two brothers sell and repair sewing machines. As someone who loves sewing I was fascinated with the manual sewing machines they sold. I decided to buy one and have it sent to me in Australia. I imagined my grandchildren one day may enjoy using it. This purchase forged a friendship with the brothers and I was invited to their home for a meal on the last day of Eid.

It was a public holiday and the bazaar was closed when one of the brothers and his sister called for me in their car. We drove some miles out to a residential area below the hills surrounding Quetta city. I was received with great enthusiasm by their father and mother and siblings. A delicious feast of a meal was served and we sat on traditional mattresses reclining against soft, silken cushions.

This family were Punjabis, many of whom live in Quetta. I was told that forty years before many Punjabi people migrated to the province of Baluchistan for employment. One of the reasons for conflict in Quetta is the hostility of original Baluch residents who resent the Punjabis. An informal political group called Baluch Separatists constantly plot against the Punjabis and take responsibility for many of the deaths in this capital. I found this family so warm and inquisitive as to why I had come to Pakistan. The daughter spoke fluent English in her questioning me. I was free to explain my faith and in answer to the why, I simply said:

> *"Because I know for certain I am loved by God. I am a Christian and I believe in Jesus His Son. I want to help the children who are Autistic. I want to establish a clinic for them in the Christian Hospital"*

The father expressed great respect for the doctors in the Christian Hospital as he had had vital surgery performed by Dr. Pont an English surgeon who had worked there with his wife an Obstetrician Dr. Molly Pont. When I told him that I was staying in what had been Dr Pont's residence he was overjoyed. He knew Dr. Pont and his wife were Christians and while he and his family were of a different faith, he held a true affection for them. The family allowed me to pray for them when I was leaving. The mother presented me with an exquisite length of embroidered fabric.

While from them I received such a welcome, in another instance from others it was not so.

One damp and cold Sunday afternoon, I decided to go out with my camera to capture the distant mountains half-shrouded in a delicate mist. I walked down a road by the canal near our compound and ducked the muddy potholes in the road. I was holding up my camera to photograph the distant mauve-veiled peaks, when a Hummer four-wheel drive zoomed up from the opposite direction and stopped suddenly. The driver rolled down his window and in a rage said:

"What you do?"

He was a rich man in the finest garb, his white shirt and pristine white silk turban displayed his superiority. He had three companions with him dressed in similar finery. I simply held up my camera and put my hands up in a peak like a mountain and spoke their word meaning *"Beautiful"*.

I then said: *"Salaam my friend, Peace"*. He snorted with fury as he wound up his window and drove off at high speed. I strolled further down the street, and enjoyed viewing the cafes with people sitting drinking coffee and engaging in conversation. No one else seemed to mind me walking around their streets. I turned into the Afghan quarter where I felt more comfortable. I had been accepted there before without hostility so I continued my stroll.

On returning, I walked back by way of the Canal Road that I had come. I could only walk on the road as the footpath had a barrier around it, as it had caved in. I looked up and could see the same Hummer four-wheel drive was returning, coming in the opposite direction. As it neared me, the driver turned the vehicle directly at me, pressing his foot on the accelerator, roaring towards me at high speed. I felt the wind of its wheels as I jumped aside into a muddy puddle. I am certain an angel must have lifted me, swiftly and lightly into the mud without slipping. My foot was securely kept. Had I slipped, I would have come under the wheels of his vehicle. A lame man on the roadside was holding out his hand for money. I shook my head and said: "Come, Come" putting my hand through his arm to help him limp away with me. A gun shot ricocheted against a wall close-by. I was warned. I was not welcome there.

Was the richly dressed turbaned driver a Baluch Separatist? Or was he a warlord, many of whom live in Quetta. They live exceedingly well, off the opium trade. They are referred to as the drug mafia. I do not know the answer except that he wanted me dead. Was the gunshot not merely a warning, but one that was aimed at me from his speeding vehicle and missed? Only God knows the answer. My camera and the fact I was a Westerner must have caused him to consider me a threat. The apparent coincidence of the Hummer returning as I was, suggested he must have waited for me on my return to run me over. I thanked God, our heavenly Father and protector who had delivered me from what I believe was intended death.

Others welcomed me, particularly in the Afghan quarter. I was offered the traditional gesture of a cup of tea as I was chatting to an Afghan naan bread maker. I was intrigued as he tossed the circular dough against the wall of his floor oven, the hot coals reflected in his fine Tajik face. He had a joy about him, a satisfaction he was contributing to the well-being of the many Afghans in his neighbourhood. Through an interpreter I was told he came every weekend to Quetta from Afghanistan, simply to make naan bread for his Afghan brothers and sisters living out of their homeland. An intense loyalty inspired him.

He was overjoyed when I told him through an interpreter, I had many Afghan friends in Australia. I told him I taught them English.

The one who interpreted for me, told me the Afghans resent the fact, that when the Durand Line was set, establishing the border between their country and Pakistan, an unjust judgement was made. They believe that much of the land was robbed from them, and great areas of Baluchistan in fact was their land by rights. It was an episode of history with which I was not familiar, but I could see it was one over which they anguished.

I continued my strolls through the marketplace whenever I had some spare hours from the meetings. I enjoyed capturing on camera the distinct energy with which the traders unloaded their wares from the donkey-drawn drays There were carpets, clothes, bed ware and saucepans weighed on scales determining their weight and cost, jewellery and fine ribbons for the home sewers, personal items as well as shop windows laden with all kinds of pastries.

The open naan bakeries with the distinct fired oven in the floor were continuously busy.

The hungry were ever-present, reaching out their hands for money. I made the mistake of handing them a few rupees, until

I was cautioned in doing that. They waited in the early mornings for me to come out of our hospital compound gates. There was such a crowd of them, the security men had to ask them to go away. It would have been wiser of me to go to the naan-bread shop and purchase enough bread for the security men to hand out and satisfy them. In some cases I was told, that any money I gave them would have been for drugs. Sad ones, without hope of deliverance.

One could see those addicted, crumpled up in a busy street, sometimes crying or groaning. The same despair was reflected in a crowd milling around the canal opening from the tunnel under our hospital compound. They were waiting for the boats to come through with contraband goods. For the addicts it was for their drugs.

I had come to Quetta, laden with gifts for my Hazara friends, the family, who I had visited on my first trip to Baluchistan. Sadly, Kumiko told me I was not able to visit them this time around, as the road to Hazaratown had become so dangerous with target shooting by extremists happening daily. It was too hazardous. She called them by phone to let them know of the gifts waiting for them.

On a sunny Sunday afternoon, a yellow Hazara cab pulled up outside the cottage where I was staying, and out stepped Joya, their son. He had come as a surprise for me, when he found out I was in the city. It was a joyous re-union. More than that, he wanted to introduce me to his wife-to-be. We walked down the driveway around the cottages and there sitting under a tree was a beautiful young woman who he planned to marry. He pleaded for me to come to the engagement celebration to be held the following

Sunday. I had to tell him I was not able to come, as by then I would be in Lahore for a conference.

He was disappointed.

Engagement for an Afghan is a very solemn event. A legal contract is drawn up, and signed by both parties. It has to be upheld. If broken, it calls for a reprisal by the offended family. These offences can cause blood feuds which are upheld for generations in some cases. I was sorry I could not be present but gave him the gifts I had brought for his family.

The days left to me in Quetta were quickly passing. I still waited for the final Agreement for the Autistic Centre to be completed. To fill in the hours I took many strolls through the laneways. On one such stroll, I smiled at a woman opening her door with her cluster of full shopping bags at her feet.

"May I take your photo?" I asked. She replied with a willing smile, which was a fresh response. Most women in this culture had refused. She invited me into her home. I was ushered into a ground floor room and her daughters came with a cup of green tea.

They asked me many questions as to how I came to be in their city? I explained I was working with the Christian Hospital with a hope of helping children with Autism. I was grateful they could understand English and responded so warmly. One daughter with a child, expressed her gratitude for the doctor at the Christian Hospital who attended her in the monitoring of her pregnancy and finally delivered her of a healthy baby. After this initial welcome I was invited to return for dinner the following evening.

Come the arranged time, I was taken upstairs to where the family lived. As is their custom we sat on the floor around an array of home-cooked exotic curries with side dishes and lots of chatter.

Their son now took place of the father who had recently passed away. He explained his mother's sorrow, and theirs. They were an educated family with the son now in business and the unmarried daughter still at university. Another daughter had recently married. As is their custom, she becomes solely a member of her husband's family and is not allowed a visit from her mother. She can go to her mother's house, but not vice versa. It is a deep relinquishment when a daughter marries.

It was an honour to be with them and to be given their trust to share so much of their lives.

It was midnight when I suggested I should be going, but not before asking them would they appreciate me praying for them? They chorused "Yes". I explained my Father in heaven's love for them, and compassion in their fresh grief at the loss of a husband and a father.

Tears came to the widow's eyes. I prayed then to our heavenly Father for her as a widow and His Fathering of them, in all the detail of their lives.

It was a dark quiet street we entered for the walk back to the Hospital, the son accompanying me. The shops were all closed, except for the ovens going in the baker's shop. The men crouched around the furnace in the floor, thrusting the dough on a long fork into the flames. With a pile of fresh naan bread at their feet, their faces glowed in the light of the flames. I had seen them every day and said hello, for five weeks. They called to me when they saw me in the dark street at such a late hour and waved with smiles. My days in Quetta were quickly closing, so their gestures gave me a sweet memory of my days in Mission Road.

21.

RELINQUISHING

The time to leave Quetta had come, but not before being invited to a luncheon to celebrate 4,000 babies having been born since the inception of the Obstetric Ward.

There was no such facility until 1995 when Dr. Molly Pont, an Obstetrician and Gynaecologist, came with her husband, an Orthopaedic Surgeon, from the U.K. Dr. Molly Pont and her husband, thereafter, came for 9 months of each year, for 14 years.

Now most of the Obstetricians/Gynaecologists in Quetta had been trained by her. These doctors are held in high esteem, which reflects Dr. Molly Pont's teaching skill, and the Lord who brought them to Quetta. It was a delightful celebration with fine food suiting the occasion.

It was a last-minute shopping trip out with Kumiko before she and I left for the conference.

In her small Suzuki van we made our way down a main road encircling the city. We waited at an intersection for the traffic

policeman to give us the go-ahead. In the outside lane we waited
to turn right. No cars were behind us. Sitting in the long back seat
against the length of the van, I looked back and could see a car at
a distance coming at reckless speed in our otherwise empty lane. I
thought it could be a suicide bomber as that is how they travel. A
collision was inevitable. I lay down and let go, calling out *"God!"* in
surrender to Him, believing I would not survive the impact. The
car hit our van with such force, throwing me on the floor. Kumiko
stunned, stalled the engine and just sat in shock.

"What is it? What happened?" She was totally disorientated. The
impact had thrown the other car onto the median strip, in a total
wreckage. Their driver and passengers were laughing manically as
if on drugs. Kumiko was sitting staring ahead. I needed to show
her how to start the van again. Her memory had been momentarily taken. The traffic policeman waved us on in agitation. Kumiko
after some time 'came to' and got the van going so we could turn
right, and park in a suitable spot. Both of us still shaking, got out
to see what damage there was. All our van suffered was a broken
tail- light and a small dent.

God had kept us from serious injury. It was yet another deliverance by our heavenly Father.

The day had come to set off for Lahore for our Mission organisation's annual Conference.

Before leaving for the conference, I had the joy of filling in
by hand, the final draft of the submission for the Australian Aid
Grant. Only one costing was to be found for a particular item in
the Builder's specification. The Medical Director assured me he
would let me know once it had been sent. Each delay had had a
divine purpose, as essential voices were able to contribute to the

submission. I needed to forego my planned trip to the Australian Embassy in Islamabad. I also needed to relinquish my concerns, and trust Jesus that in His time, it would be finalised.

Kumiko and I flew into Lahore in the evening. It was a different entry this time. We were smoothly driven in a late model car, along a newly built freeway. It was in stark contrast to my first wild entry into the city a year before. Then it was through the back streets of the markets at midnight in a battered little car. No close calls with donkeys or motor bikes this time.

It was a hearty welcome into the company of fellow-workers as we met in the Retreat Centre for the Conference. Three Australian brothers in Christ, came with our Australian Director, who gave the teaching for the conference. It was good to hear a familiar accent.

The sessions in the Conference proved searching and refining. We all shared our stories of how the Lord had led us over the past year. I shared with thanksgiving.

God had so wonderfully provided for me in gifts from my church family when illness and lack of finances contested my return to Pakistan. Their encouragement and support was a deep affirmation to keep going.

It had been a difficult year. A false accusation had been made concerning my first trip to Pakistan. It came in a written report just as I was planning to return for this second trip. It had no identity to it. I was not given any opportunity to address that before leaving Pakistan, the year before. It had really disturbed my fellow churchmen back in Australia. I was completely in the dark and could not see how that accusation was true in any way. I was crushed by it and had I not been taking a young companion with me, I believe I would have not gone through with my plans to return. We were booked to leave in ten days' time. I did not want to disappoint my younger companion. It caused so much confusion and unnecessary anxiety in my leaders back home, a shadow came over my soul. The sorrow of this incident hit me with fresh pain in the conference.

I took a break in between conference sessions and walked along the dirty, muddy, smelly street with motor bikes revving and twisting to avoid the cars and fragile rickshaws. Kids in the dump-space of a park were practicing cricket around the heaps of rubbish. I needed to settle the issues in my soul. I needed to forgive the one who had not brought their accusation to me face-to-face in the shelter of wise and careful leadership. I had no benefit of explaining or being given biblical counsel. Tears are good when no tangible comfort is forthcoming. I kept walking and further on, entered the grounds of the Presbyterian Cathedral, still being built.

I needed to take shelter from my own thoughts. I could not fathom why God would ask me, of all people to come to a place like Pakistan, where people were so needy and hurting?

There were so many servants more resilient than I was. I was offered a broken chair to sit on, by the builder when he saw me enter the worksite. Sitting under a tree with the widest branches was cooling. I was broken in spirit. I even asked the Muslim builder, who had pulled up a chair next to me, what did he think God was like? I was losing a grip on faith and in despair. Strangely, this led to a probing exchange with him, and I explained to him, who I believed God was and Jesus, His likeness. I also confessed to the builder, that I thought God chose unlikely people like me to come and serve people in Pakistan. My nose was running, so the builder probably agreed with me. Kindly, he let me cry, but not before letting me pray for him based on his searching words as our conversation closed.

He welcomed this. By that I was comforted.

Just as I was thinking of returning to the conference centre, the minister of the Presbyterian Church strolled up and introduced himself with a smile. Recognising I was a visitor, he wanted to show me the cathedral that was almost completed. But first, he took me to introduce me to his wife, and show me where they lived. I needed to be told of, and understand someone else's life.

He pointed to their ruined home in the grounds of the cathedral. It had been rendered uninhabitable in a deluge of rain. Below and beside their home was a deep culvert where the rain-water had caused a landslide. A complete wall of their home had been wrenched away by flood waters, and the inside of their home open to view. He had lost many of his precious books in a treasured library. He nevertheless, was calm and uncomplaining. He explained that he and his wife were camped under the portico at the back of the new cathedral. There was no door for privacy. They were completely open to the weather.

There his wife was tidying their shelter of improvised screens for their beds, with cooking pots and kitchenware in clusters on the ground. When introduced she greeted me with a radiant smile. I marvelled at their cheerfulness in living in such poor circumstances until their home could be rebuilt.

He took me into the newly built cathedral with fresh arches of timber reaching into a generous ceiling. Tall windows invited the light. I asked him could he pray for me? I explained I was finding it difficult to hear God in the midst of pain. This he did wisely, lovingly and knowingly. He then invited me to stay. I sat in a back pew while men, mostly young, came in for a lunchtime service. Their unaccompanied voices rang to the rafters in worship. It was a restoring breath from heaven.

The new cathedral is a resounding witness to Christ, built after years of struggle when the old one had to be demolished. Driving in from the airport at night, we saw, illuminated and reaching into the evening sky, at the highest point of the roofline, two hands, palms together in prayer. It reflected the desperate cry of the Lord's children in this city. Believers here, live in a contrary spiritual world.

22.

RE-VISITED

As the conference closed, it was time for workers to return to their individual locations. I was to go with our Ethiopian brother and sister, and their daughter. We set off at night for the 10- hour coach drive southward, back to Rahim Yar Khan. I was eager to go back to the place where my time in Pakistan had begun 12 months before. As well as hoping to visit the School where I had taught, plans were made to re-visit some of the villages and communities who had been ravaged by the catastrophic flood.

It was in the early hours of the morning when we three adults and one child, plus a pile of luggage fitted into a small rickety rickshaw and rocked and swayed our way down the laneway of mission headquarters. Nathaniel the gatekeeper was asleep under the cool of the stars, in the courtyard. He gave me a royal welcome back to Rahim Yar Khan as he opened the large metal gates. Hospitality sparkles in this part of the world. The Pakistani staff are a lesson in faithfulness.

While I was sitting in the cool of the garden after sun-up, Husheed the housekeeper, came through the front gate and see-ing me, opened her arms and we ran towards each other. She is a valued keeper of the houses, and everyone's needs. We were so excited to see each other, as with Javed the driver. He and his wife and children welcomed me with a garland of roses and a fine meal. Fahdya, the boy who sweeps the Mission compound was no longer a boy but a lanky young man. We shook hands. They still smiled at moments they recalled from my previous visit.

One they remember, was when I was wanting some fresh chicken pieces. It got lost in translation. Javed relayed to the one who was doing the shopping for me, as a request for 'live chicken pieces'. I remember laughing until I ached. When I got my breath back I said: "*No!...just chicken pieces!*" It is now a reference for them if ever they have something in English that gets scrambled, it is referred to as 'another chicken story'. I seem to have given them plenty of laughs which was good, after a sober week of conference when my courage was wavering.

I sat down to a welcome meal with my Ethiopian brother and sister. We mulled over what the past year had brought in God. There was so much to tell. They promised to take me back into the communities which had been destroyed by the treacherous flood. Regular trips had been made by them into these people groups. They had much to tell of what God had done, but I had to wait. First there were shorter trips to be taken closer to the city of Rahim Yar Khan.

My Ethiopian brother took me to a gathering of Pakistani pas-tors and house church leaders and told them of the prayer group in my home, back in Australia, over the past months. They were grateful and asked me there and then, to pray for them which I did, with the help of an interpreter.

They represent 26 house Churches in the Punjab and Sindh regions. They meet three times a month to study the Scriptures and to pray together. They pray with such fervour and passion, a reflection of being a minority under surveillance in this culture.

They constantly need to be on their guard. They are deeply dependant on the Lord.

I received with joy some news from one of the pastors, where we had distributed quilts and warm clothes after the flood. I asked about a young woman who was suffering from tuberculosis at the time we visited the year before. Then, I had been asked to pray for her.

She and I sat on a log, I put my arms around my young sister in Christ, and asked for the hand of Jesus to touch her and if He was willing, to heal her, in His mercy. The pastor told me with a bright smile that she was completely healed and really well. *Thank You Jesus!*

There was double reason for thanksgiving. Four months after my return from that first trip I developed a troubling dry cough. I had to quarantine. It was suspected I may have caught the tubercular infection from my close contact. Wonderfully I was cleared after being tested at the TB clinic in one of our major hospitals. They found the immunisation I had received as a high school student over 50 years before was very active as anti-bodies. I had not succumbed to the disease. Again, *Thank You Jesus!* I recalled how when I prayed for the young woman, the power of God hit us with such force, we both jumped. A strange but extravagant gesture from Him. Now she was whole.

As a new day came at mission headquarters, we piled into the four-wheel drive, and set off for a farming village not far from Rahim Yar Khan. We travelled with a visiting Korean medical team. We bumped our way through dirt and potholes, the Koreans joyously squeezed into the back seat. They had an armed policeman assigned for their protection, sitting in the back of the truck. He seemed to enjoy the ride as well as the praise and worship when we arrived. He dutifully stood guard over us with a smile. After giving a bible talk, translated into the Pakistan language of Urdu, the Korean medicos sang worship songs to Jesus in their mother-tongue. It was then that the clinic was open.

A long queue of people to be seen by the doctors, snaked out into the church yard, with screams of pain from some and consternation in others waiting to be seen. Children of the village were sitting in the shade of the church. The children loved hearing that I came from a distant land called Australia. I told them some of the things that make our land distinct.

Most of all I told them I loved Jesus. They listened intently. When the screams had died down from the people receiving medical treatment, we set off back to the headquarters in Rahim Yar Khan city.

I received with eagerness an invitation to visit the English Allied Model School where I had taught English. It was a delightful re-union with the students I had taught, at what now was the opening of the new School building. Having taught the previous year in rooms under construction and stepping over building rubble to enter, I was now a guest-of-honour. I was invited to the podium for the official Dedication, Declaration and Prayer.

A garland of roses was placed around my neck.

The school is a splendid building, with each class now having their own room. There were newly enrolled girls, which evidenced their fresh intention to encourage female education.

It was an honour to be there for this day. My students smiled and waved to me in joy that I was there. Thirty or so guests sat down to a celebratory luncheon. I was humbled when they asked me to pray the grace over the meal. It was a privilege I was given.

Another joy in my days in Rahim Yar Khan, was to meet each morning with two Pakistan staff members in the Mission Office. We studied the Word together and then had a time of prayer. For the three weeks I was there, our friendship grew in trust, and in sharing personal needs, and the needs of the work, reaching into distant zones of the Punjab and beyond. It was to these villages that at last a trip was to be undertaken with my Ethiopian brother and sister. We were to return to the area ravaged by flood the year before.

Our able Pakistani driver who had taken us twelve months before into the treacherously flooded villages, was now eager to take me back. Since my last trip he had come into a firm faith in Christ through the careful tuition of our Ethiopian evangelist. He had a new joy and was taking an active part in preaching trips to the villages. Because Urdu was his mother-tongue he did the Bible readings. He was no longer simply a skilled driver, but a valued outreach companion.

Others had worked tirelessly to help in the restoration and the sharing of the gospel to those whose livelihood had been robbed by the flood the year before. For me, the recovery was unknown. I had only seen the villages in ruins.

We entered the home described in my story "Room in the Dark". Just as before, we sat in the dimly lit room, on the huge bed, surrounded by the children of the extended family.

This time, joy was in the widow's face. She had come to know Christ. What a difference in her demeanour. It was her younger brother who had first brought the knowledge of the gospel to this family. He now introduced me to his future bride, who also had come to faith. The wedding was to come in the following year. His younger sister of 12 yrs. old had also become a Christian. What a different household welcomed me this time.

You may recall my describing how the woman who was tormented and oppressed by evil, had come to peace after she was prayed for. Now, on our second visit someone went to let her know we were there. A happy commotion could be heard, as feet quickly made the steps up to the room where we were sitting. I looked up. I gasped. Was it really her?

I was speechless. She smiled the most open smile when she saw me. What had been a gaunt and lean expression of ugly fear had been replaced by a wide radiance, of full, healthy cheeks. Jesus had set her free. He had brought deliverance and healing to her whole being. She glowed. How could one ever doubt His power? Her arms were outstretched to me in joy. She wanted to hold onto me. It was a hold of thanksgiving, for both of us.

After lots of chatter, and welcome tea, we reluctantly waved goodbye, and set off down the laneways, to the valley below. The children came with us, leading the way. Others joined along. They grabbed my hands, giggling in delight. They were taking me back to where, on my first visit, I had been given a chair to sit on, and a dried book from the floodwaters, to read to them. That day I had been surrounded by angry men of the community, and we had had to make a swift departure because of their and others' hostility. Now the sun shone on freshly restored homes. Some were still being completed, but able to be lived in.

The girl who had brought me the book to read a year before, now proudly took me to her restored home. What a welcome I received.

Chai was freshly prepared for me and brought with great ceremony. I don't enjoy chai usually, but that day it was delicious! It was served with such love and welcome. I was staggered that they had not forgotten me. I had certainly not forgotten them. In gestures of simple English which the daughter understood, I offered to pray for them. What a privilege to pray for this family and yes, a second family I visited. From a people, twelve months before who had so intimidated the World Health workers, as to prevent them unloading their relief supplies, now welcomed me into their homes. They smiled with gratitude, that I had come back to see them and their hard work to make new homes. I prayed for the gospel to be freely available to them, that they would have a revelation of Jesus. Our Father has heard those prayers. He will answer.

We set off by foot to another area on the edge of the town towards the home of the Hindu Guru. In the intervening year, my Ethiopian brother and sister had made many visits teaching him from the Scriptures. They had emailed me when I was home in Australia, to tell me with great joy, that the Guru had come to faith in Christ. It was a happy prospect to see the family again.

You will remember I am sure, me telling you of his son lying on the camp bed, having suffered a serious illness. From this he was left brain-injured, had lain prone for three years, unable to sit up or speak or feed himself. As we walked up the slope to their home, along a grassy path, and coming to the rise, I gasped in wonder. There again on the camp bed, the same boy, this time, sitting up and drinking from a cup he was holding to his mouth, all unassisted. His torso was strong and his shoulders erect.

"Remember me?" I yelped in joy.

He responded with an exuberant smile and a joyous laugh. I spoke gently, telling him, with interpreting help from my Ethiopian sister in Christ, just how wonderful it was to see him, looking so well. He agreed in excitement. Jesus' healing mercy had ministered an extraordinary change in him. I hugged him with thanksgiving. My sister and I then decided to pray for his legs to be given life. I turned his body around so his legs were over the edge of the bed. With both of us holding them, we prayed again for the Lord's healing virtue to give him mobility. I longed for him to have the opportunity for physiotherapy, which would have surely been of great benefit. I imagined a walking frame may have helped to get his muscles working correctly, or callipers for support. No such facility was available in this remote village. We prayed that the Lord's mercy would overrule such disadvantage. His shining face was evidence of Jesus' powerful presence with this young man.

From later enquiries I made, no updates could be secured as to how he was progressing.

Our heavenly Father knows. The most recent updates concerning the father of the boy, was that the former Hindu Guru was suffering severe persecution as a follower of Christ.

Prayer is our resort, believing God keeps His promise of protection for those who truly call out to Him. Such are our prayers for this once leading Hindu, but now a brother in Christ.

Our next village visit was to a community who had once resided in a deep valley. When the treacherous waters had overflowed from the Indus River, in a deluge, nothing was left of their dwellings. They had now been re-located on a hill, out of reach of any future flooding. This was formerly a Hindu community which had received the gospel of Jesus, and been transformed. My Ethiopian brother and sister who had brought me to see this new community told me of the joy with which they had received the Good News when they had preached to them.

Women had thrown away their Hindu amulets. Every vestige of worship to the Hindu gods had been destroyed. It was a remarkable witness to the power of the gospel which had totally changed this small community. I thought of the words to describe Zion, a city set on a hill. It was a miniature Zion now residing on higher ground, under the blessing of Father God. They had been receiving regular visits from our Ethiopian brother and sister who taught them the Word of God. We had a time of teaching that day, and I clearly recall their shining faces.

As days passed back at Rahim Yar Khan, the season of Muhurrum returned. On the mission compound where I was staying, at strategic prayer time for Muslims, the Shi-ite policeman keeping guard would put his rifle aside and take fine branches from the small trees in the garden. He then paced up and down the driveway, whipping himself and chanting the prayers of mourning for the Cousin of Mohammad as is their custom.

At midnight, one could hear the people pacing up and down the laneway at the back of the compound where we were sleeping. A rhythmic thudding of leather on flesh, vibrated with their chant, whipping themselves as an offering for the death of the Cousin of

Mohammed. One saw people in the street whipping themselves, in grief over the days of the season of Muhurrum.

It was a rich time for these weeks, back in the territory of flood relief the year before. I could clearly see what God had done in the intervening season. Fellowship with fellow-workers was sweet. It did come to an end and I packed my bags for home.

At Rahim Yar Khan airport, an airport officer asked me to open my suitcase. He rummaged through everything, throwing it out of the suitcase in disarray. On discovering my Bible and holding it up he spat out the words:

"*Are you a Christian?*" to which I answered:

"*Yes, I am*". With scorn, he threw my Bible back into the luggage and proceeded to stuff back, without care, all the things he had thrown out. I begged him to let me repack the suitcase, as I could see it wouldn't be possible to close it, the way he was shoving everything in. I had not had anyone before, question me at an airport about my faith. Other things they have puzzled over but never my Bible. I flew out of Rahim Yar Khan, and connected with a flight the next day to Australia.

PART 3
2012

23.

HOMECOMING

It was really good to be home with loved ones. Holiday times allowed me to spend precious hours with them. I was looking forward to seeing my church family, and re-assuring them I was well, and an intended task had been accomplished. I was to be disappointed. I came into the gathering of my fellowship that day to discover much pain had been endured while I was away. Our church had experienced a disagreement at executive level and now two valued ministers were departing. My brothers and sisters were numb. No one asked me how I was or seemed capable of hearing any good news from me. All there was, was a collective grief and silence.

An invitation came from friends living up North of the state. They knew I was weary and might benefit from a few days' rest. It was a welcome break. There was much to process after the intense, varied time in Pakistan. One evening I sensed it might be wise to check my email box. I puzzled over an email from Joya, the young

Hazara Afghan who had visited me at the Christian Hospital. He asked me to ring him on 'this number' which I did.

In alarm I heard him tell me he had left his home and family in Quetta. So many young men were being killed on the roads to their town, he had left, with his family's sorrowful blessing. He spoke to me from the jungle in Indonesia where with others, he was hiding.

His intention was to catch a smuggler's boat to Christmas Island with the hope of being accepted in Australia. I said with alarm:

"You will be locked up!" He was not dissuaded. I felt sick at the thought of what lay ahead. The phone call ended abruptly.

The grief lingered concerning my church family. It would take a long while for fresh hope to birth in us. Many of us decided to leave. I joined another church family who would come to be precious as well. I kept in touch with my former brothers and sisters, who, appreciated receiving updates on the news from Pakistan. They are so faithful and to this day, hold a place of respect and love in my heart. It was their prayerful and financial support which enabled me to make these journeys.

Settling back in the day-to-day, I continued to keep the Christian Hospital Autistic needs uppermost in my thoughts and prayers. I emailed the Medical Director, who said the application was still being processed by the Diocese. I also knew by news updates from Quetta, that much violence was breaking out. I read with alarm the Director of the Red Cross in that city had been kidnapped. Such an essential service was under attack. I continued to look for encouraging emails from the hospital. None came.

I rang the Medical Director, who was in surgery at the time, so it had to be brief. I asked him how the application was progressing? *"Not good in Quetta. Have you heard the news?"* was his reply.

"Yes, I have. Terrible". I answered.

The Red Cross Director who I had talked with at the dinner party that night, was killed by his kidnappers and found on the side of the road outside the city. Red Cross had removed all workers from Quetta.

"It is not good here." His voice was heavy and sad.

"I understand." I replied.

"I must go" he quickly interjected. The phone call ended.

Weeks went by and I looked for any encouragement that our well-researched plans for the Autistic Centre would prevail. No emails. No clear explanation.

My concern on a daily basis was not only for those plans, but Joya's welfare. I finally received a phone call. He had arrived on Christmas Island. He seemed okay. His voice a little wistful, but hopeful. Each time he rang, I prayed for him for a strong sense of the presence of the Lord for him.

"Mum, I see Jesus! Each time I close my eyes I see His face." I was deeply encouraged and marvelled that Jesus certainly was clear to him. I was also assured concerning his well-being. His phone calls were understandably limited, being in a detention centre, but every now and then, my mobile would ring, and I would be reassured he was safe. I was careful also to ask him, how his family were coping back in Hazaratown outside Quetta.

His family found his absence almost unbearable.

Still no news came from the Christian Hospital regarding the Autistic Diagnostic & Development Centre. I was puzzled and grieved. Would all our work, our research, our discussions in the hospitals and schools come to nothing? All the trips in insecure locations, be wasted? One email came from the Medical Director, in response to my queries, telling me that there was a general exit of Medical specialists from Quetta.

Kidnapping of valuable Doctors, with the demands for ransom was becoming too frequent to sustain.

Enquiring emails came from the Australian Embassy in Islamabad, asking where were the Application documents for the Australian Aid Grant? I could give them no rational answer, except that the insecure situation in Quetta was holding up the process. I was embarrassed, as they had short-listed the hospital for a Grant for the Autistic children out of hundreds of applicants. My disappointment was deep.

The weeks, then the months passed. The year was one where nothing was stable.

No developments came concerning the Autistic Centre, in Quetta. My church family who had been so faithful, no longer existed in its whole. Many had chosen to leave and go to other churches. My concerns had come to be focused on Joya, who now was transferred to Wickham Point Detention Centre out of Darwin, then lastly after many months to Weipa in Northern Queensland. One surprising phone call from him told me he was being released. It was the first happy news of the year.

I waited at the airport, to welcome him. It was a tender moment as he came through the exit doorway with his fellow detainees. Each had their refugee number on a sticker on their chest. Each face reflected a fragility of having spent months in a confined supervised enclosure. We hugged before he boarded a bus for the accommodation provided by the Red Cross in Sydney.

I was exercised in my mind and heart as to whether to invite Joya to come and live with me. It seemed a softer entry to his new land than living in an institutional setting. I was diffident not knowing him well, though having been in his family's home in Quetta.

When praying about this the Lord reminded me of many years before when I was married, I suffered a miscarriage of a deeply longed-for child. I wanted a son and hoped this baby would be a fulfillment. At a conference I attended not long after this loss, I received prayer from an Afro-American lady. She prayed for me to be comforted and said after deep thought:

"I think there is a son for you" She then wept, denoting some sorrow. I didn't fully comprehend.

Now in this moment of endeavouring to hear God's wisdom on inviting Joya to come and live with me, I sensed the Lord say:

"This is the son". I decided to invite him to live with me.

On visiting him in the Red Cross facility he agreed very eagerly. I was glad I could contribute to his settlement in his new country.

As he lived with me I learnt that he was born the exact month, the exact year, my longed-for baby would have been born. His mother told him thick snow surrounded them the day he arrived in the early month of the new year. Is it cause for wonder at God's knowledge of us in the smallest detail of our lives? That day I was prayed for, so many years ago, a baby soon to be born far away in the hills of Ghazni, Afghanistan would be His answer. Now for this season, he was to be a son to me. A son with tears.

I listened to his story of his journey from Malaysia to Indonesia where only a few of his original companions escaped arrest. Twenty-three had set off in a group, but only four made it to Christmas Island. The rest were incarcerated in Malaysia's prison.

Some were to be there for five years.

He became troubled, recounting to me the sea voyage from Indonesia in an insecure boat, crammed with refugees. Standing was the only option, as there was no room for sitting, so crowded was the boat. After two days and three nights they still had not reached the Island. Vomit and excrement was prolific without adequate toilets. Water was in short supply. They were taking a lot longer than they should have.

It was on their third night at sea that Joya became agitated and begged the captain for information:

"We should be there!"

He did this, repeatedly, returning to the deck and crying out to God for help. The boat was plied in the same direction with no sight of land. The captain showed no sign of understanding or wanting to understand. The boat was breaking up. They had crammed all available clothing into the cavities. He was sure they would die, when the lights of a small Australian Navy aircraft came from the distant night horizon.

It circled their boat. *"Turn around, you are going the wrong way"* was amplified. *"Follow us"* came the repeated call. Joya with his limited language, relayed this to the captain. The aircraft circled for them to get the right bearings and flew ahead of them. In the promise of a new day, the breaking boat with its fragile cargo limped into Christmas Island.

They were immediately taken on board a naval ship and thermal blankets thrown around them. They waited for the dawn to rise when the port would be opened. Joya wept as he recounted this. He often cried in his sleep and I wondered if he was again on that dangerous journey heading out into the depths of the Indian Ocean. God had answered his cries for mercy. *Thank You Father!*

Now settled into my home, together we read Luke's Gospel, each morning. Joya's English comprehension in reading and speaking was comparatively good. Every morning we started the day with prayer. We learnt how to consider each other and what were the necessary steps for him to take to learn English competently for seeking employment. He registered with a local facility teaching English and went off daily to his class.

His fiancée was also a deep concern for us, so necessary enquiries were made with the relevant agencies. It was a learning process for both of us. It seemed that maximum opportunity would be given for his spouse to join him, if they were married. We kept the hope alive, that he would be able to one day go back and be married. It didn't seem easily realisable.

A delight of our time while he lived with me, was, that now he could speak freely of his coming to faith in Christ. As a keen volley-ball player, at the age of fourteen, he was playing a game in his refugee town in Pakistan, when after the game an Afghan man approached him. They chatted for a while, and the man explained he was a Christian, and invited Joya to his home. From then on Joya visited him regularly where he was taught the scriptures. After four months Joya gave his life to Christ. He was the only one that he knew of in his Muslim family, who had come to faith.

He told his father he no longer was going to the mosque with him as he was now a Christian. Wonderfully his father was not angry. He gave him freedom to meet in secret with other believers in his hometown.

Joya told me about a Canadian missionary to Quetta who had given his family great assistance when they first escaped from Afghanistan. She knew his family well, and though now she was retired back in Canada, still maintained contact with them. I was brought into their circle of friendship. By email I told her, Joya was a Christian, and had come as a refugee to live with me in Australia. She was joyful about this news and wrote in an email::

"Now I know he is a Christian I have something to tell Joya". I promised we would ring her, which we did.

It was then, she was able to speak to him of his older brother who had been an interpreter with the U.S. Army in Afghanistan. He had been killed when out on patrol. She told Joya the wonderful news, that his brother, was also, a believer in Christ. She had helped disciple him. He in fact was such a lover of Jesus, it was obvious to all those who had known him and served with him. Joya, on hearing this, handed the phone back to me and putting his head in his hands, sobbed. He had so loved his brother and knew him as such a loving brother. He was already broken-hearted over his death. Neither had had the opportunity to speak of their faith to each other. The age difference meant they were apart for many years, when his brother was serving in conflict. That, and the restraints within a Muslim context had rendered it difficult to communicate freely.

Joya's tears were replaced with joy, that as Christians knowing we would one day be resurrected with Christ, he would see his brother again. The Canadian missionary posted to him some letters his brother had written to her over the years. His faith spoke so clearly from his words.

By a strange blessing of preparation, I could recall some years earlier, while watching the evening news in my own home in Australia, one report of the conflict in Afghanistan spoke of a deadly strike on U.S. soldiers. The U.S. General lamented that they had lost their most gifted Afghan interpreter. He described him as a man of fine character. They showed a portrait of this Afghan interpreter, and I remember thinking, *what a beautiful face.* Joya showed me a photo of his loved brother, and I realised, it was that same face, shown on the evening news, that had arrested my attention. I now knew that the life of Christ in him, accounted for that *beautiful face, and his fine character.*

He had secured a job for Joya with the U.S. Army, working in Logistics. On that fateful day of the attack on the U.S. soldiers out on patrol, a phone call came, requesting Joya to come to see his brother. He was directed to the Medical Clinic, to be informed his brother was dead. He had the terrible responsibility of ringing his parents to inform them. He accompanied his brother's body in the U.S. Army vehicle back to the border with Pakistan.

Joya with his brother's body was then transferred for the journey back to his home, for burial in Hazaratown. It was a responsibility of heavy weight for someone so young.

While sorrow veils this family, God had His hand on them. Their mother and father had endured not only displacement through the Taliban, but also separation from loved ones.

While they escaped from Afghanistan, a married daughter with children had stayed behind with her husband. Over the years of living in a new land, contact with each other was lost.

Joya's mother and father fretted for their daughter, and were fearfully concerned for her and her children's welfare. No news of their whereabouts could be secured, or their safety in a land oppressed by the Taliban insurgents. Time waiting, with heavy hearts, weighed heavily on them.

At this time Joya's brother, while still alive and serving as an interpreter with the U.S. Army, came to a village along with the soldiers, searching for much needed water. They came across a well, but needed a vessel to collect it. His brother, the only one speaking the Afghan language of Dari knocked on a door to ask for a container to gather the water.

A gaunt, emaciated young woman came to the door. In alarm, Joya's brother realised it was their long-lost sister. She was no longer the young woman he remembered, but he knew it was her. She was hollow, without life, deeply withdrawn. She was starving. Her husband and children had died, and now their mother appeared to have lost her mind.

She showed no recognition that he was her brother. He did not alert her, as to who he was. With the U.S. Army's assistance, she was transported to Kandahar to be given medical treatment. Her brother had her set up in accommodation, and finally after months when she was strong enough, was given safe passage back to their family in Pakistan.

Joya recounted to me, that when she arrived in their home in Pakistan, she was so out of her mind, she did not recognise any of them. She was so severely withdrawn. Slowly and tenderly his mother nursed her back to full health. Only a heavenly Father could have planned that day of rescue, when water was needed by soldiers in a remote village of Afghanistan. One of His sons was taken to the very door to discover his sister.

Many moments were shared, with Joya telling me the story of his upbringing in Afghanistan. Up to the age of 10 he attended a Madrassa. The Muslim school for boys gave little opportunity for a rounded education. The curriculum consisted mainly of Koran chants in Arabic. It wasn't until Joya's older brother then residing in Pakistan, sent him books and pencils with textbooks to learn how to read and write, and do Maths, that Joya began to truly learn. As a country boy living in the hills in the province of Gazhni, all formal education was self-taught. In the afternoons he would climb the hills with his mother, to gather green feed for their goats.

As the Taliban encroached on their village, the family escaped to Pakistan. Joya was thirteen years old. As he developed as a strong teenager in Hazaratown he proved to be an excellent volley-ball player. The Hazara team with whom he played represented the province of Baluchistan in the National Volleyball games in Lahore. They returned home triumphantly holding the National Trophy. Their joy was short-lived. Because they were despised as Hazara Afghans within Pakistan, a deadly attack came. The triumphant Hazara team's coach was shot dead as an act of hatred by the opposition.

Joya experienced extraordinary incidences of God's protection as a believer. Back in Hazaratown, after returning with his brother's body, he decided to stay home and return to High School to qualify for matriculation for university. His morning routine before school, was to go for a walk and sit in a park to pray, not far from his home. On one exceptional morning, he slept in, and so after breakfast returned to his room, to read his bible and pray. He heard several rounds of gunfire. Anxious, he went up onto the roof to see what was happening. Sixteen people in the park, where he normally would be sitting, were slaughtered by insurgents. His life had been spared.

In another instance while serving in logistics with the U.S. Army he drove over an Improvised Explosive Device hidden in the road by the Taliban. The four-wheel drive exploded in half and Joya lay on the side of the road until picked up by Army medicos.

The left side of his chest was cut open and he has a scar to this day. One eye was damaged requiring him to wear glasses to see clearly.

After his brother's death, he needed to attend to the sale of his brother's land in Herat on the western boundary of Afghanistan. The bus in which he was travelling was apprehended by the Taliban. They boarded the bus and at gunpoint ordered the Hazaras off the bus. Joya and two other men had to get out. After a heated exchange with Joya defending his reason for being on the bus, they let him re-board. The other two were taken off. Joya presumed they would have been shot. God had kept him.

While Joya was living with me in Sydney, he would go off each day to English Class. In any free moment, he enjoyed drawing. His artistic skills are considerable. While in detention, he continually drew and wrote his journal. He won an Art Award while in Wickham Point detention centre and received a monetary prize which he valued. He also has a gift in words. He read aloud to me, with translation, some of his journal entries he had made while in detention. At Wickham Point detention centre, they were housed on the coastal edge. He spoke of the 'voice of the sea'. Living in a land-locked country, Afghans hold a kind of terror of the sea, which has to be overcome living in the coastal region of Australia.

The weeks and months proved valuable time for Joya settling into his strange new land.

After repeated trips to the official government departments, one triumphant day he was granted a Permanent Visa. He could now safely reside in Australia. We celebrated with a lunch in the city. All that he had gone through to get to this point, made that meal deeply significant. As we walked down George Street in the city, he stood still and looked up at the skyscrapers of city office blocks and said in wonder:

"I'm a boy from Gahzni !"

Pleas came from his fiancée and family, hopeful that now he had been given permanency in Australia, one day they may see his face again. He yearned for them, just as they did for him. We prayed and asked God, was there any possibility of him returning to be married? God had planned for it. A provision of finances at last made it possible for him to return to his family for a visit, and to be married. Joya's family begged him to bring me with him. I was reluctant to go. My two visits to Quetta had been so full and demanding within the violent setting. My original concern for the Autistic children was bearing little fruit. I was dismayed that as yet nothing had been accomplished for them.

After, thinking, discussing and praying about returning, I at last said "Yes". I would accompany Joya back to his home. It was necessary now to gain a visa, not only for him but for me. Our trips to the relevant consulate to apply for a return visit to Pakistan, proved a challenge. They understood Joya's motivation to get married, but why did I need to go?

I was applying to visit and reside in Hazaratown as a guest of his family. No Westerner had ever been allowed to stay overnight, in this besieged town, let alone reside for 6 weeks.

After a tussle of words, I was granted this unique privilege. We packed for our trip, back to Quetta, and the road trip to Hazaratown. His family were overjoyed at the anticipation of seeing him again, after so many months. They and I had met two years before when Kumiko had taken me to their home. I also hoped to visit the Christian Hospital and explore the reason for the lack of progress in the Autistic Centre project. Silence had settled into sorrow for me, that there was no communication concerning the Plans and Application for funds.

24.

WELCOME

By surprise, Joya's family were at Quetta airport to meet us. We had planned simply on getting a taxi to save them making the risky journey from their home, but there they were.

What love and longing for each other. It was good that Joya had come back. He held his elderly father for a long while, sheltering his sobs, then his mother's. His fiancée Rahima stood patiently waiting. Under the cover of darkness we were driven at high speed through the back roads to their home. Our luggage piled on the roof rack, had the seal of the dust of Quetta to show for it.

It had not been a straightforward journey from Australia to Quetta. On arrival at Islamabad airport we were detained twice under security police's pretence of supposed inadequate documents for Joya. All this for the purpose of extracting bribes from us. We refused.

The Lord gave me the words to speak. After tense, tedious debate the airport security handed back Joya's passport and let us go.

The second incident came on the busy six-lane freeway from the airport, where the police stopped our car with the same accusation. Contacts at the airport must let the police know we had come off a flight. They presume as a Westerner I had money on me. Standing on the grassy verge of the crazy traffic, close to midnight, after being awake for almost 24 hours, shouting above the noise of the traffic, with a rifle close by my face, my patience was sorely tested. Even the taxi driver joined in our defence, and they let us go.

At Quetta airport, the one place we expected difficulty, the police officer asked me to fill in a form as to my planned stay, and the date of my departure. He looked at my date, and where I planned to be staying. He was troubled and frowned.

"Oh…my dear…be careful…you are as my mother"

It was such a tender, careful remark, in contrast to the raw response in Islamabad.

Joya was weary. He was also comforted by the prayers of his believing friends back in Australia. We both sensed we were clothed in our brothers' and sisters' prayer. After an hour or so of the family surrounding him and chatting in catch-up news Joya went to stay with his fiancée's family, who lived close-by.

I was encompassed by his family and shown my room with a carefully made bed.

Everything was set out for my comfort. Joya's younger brother and sister could speak English, and made sure my needs were met.

The first morning after arrival, the family gathered with Joya and his wife-to-be, for a time of gift-giving.

On Joya's suggestion, we all joined hands as he prayed for the Lord to come with His presence and understanding. He asked our heavenly Father, for each one to know His love for them, for their salvation. It was a courageous gesture by him, as his family were of Muslim faith.

Once settled into my room I gazed around. On the wall was a framed Citation of Valour given to his brother who had been killed while serving with the U.S. Army. His C.D. player was on a shelf nearby, alongside his portrait photo. How strange and inestimable is Father God's linking together His children's lives. That night in my home in Australia, watching the news, and being arrested by the description and photo of the young Afghan interpreter killed out on patrol, I never imagined I would be staying with his family, nor in a room with his personal items on the shelf below his Citation of Valour.

Many visitors arrived, relatives and friends to welcome Joya back. He came around to his family home to welcome them. Each day I endeavoured to learn new words in my hosts' language of Hazaragi, a dialect of the Afghan language of Dari. I sat on the back porch in the sun with Joya's younger brother, while he taught me grammar, and basic verbs. I was eager to learn. Joya's mother, in the kitchen, gave me the names of the food items she was preparing. She was a good teacher. She had never had the benefit of school, so while not able to read or write her own language, she was a masterful cook. Her meals were really tasty.

Guladam the older sister still at home, also cooked. Some days I sat on the kitchen floor with her, as she stirred the pot simmering with meat and vegetables over the primus flames. She had a wonderful smile. She prepared special tomato and green leaf salads for me, knowing that is what I appreciated. On occasions, a magnificent Afghan pressure cooker was brought out to prepare a lamb dish. How the stock was created, I do not know, but it was delicious.

Every day they were busy, cleaning, preparing food, baking bread, washing clothes, or doing handiwork or turning the wheel on their manual sewing machine. I loved watching Guladam's hands work busily with such rhythm in fine thread. Her crocheted lace was so delicate. Joya's mother produced wondrously colourful embroidery in traditional Hazara design. His younger sister attended school in the afternoon, and when not helping with house chores, was studying earnestly. She appreciated me helping her with her English, as did his younger brother.

The courtyard of their home was a feast for the eyes. A range of vegetables were growing, surrounded by a tall fence, adorned with roses. On the roof garden, green herbs flourished. One could imagine their farming hands labouring so prosperously in their homeland. Here, as refugees, far from Gahzni, Afghanistan they created in miniature, a bounty of vegetables, fruit and flowers.

The older daughter prepared the Naan dough for baking. Crouching on a cloth on the floor, she worked the dough and then, after its rising, rolled out meticulously the shape of the bread for her mother to slap the dough into the oven. I watched them intently work in harmonious rhythm. With a large basket of fresh Naan covered in a cloth, Joya's mother set off on her rounds to various households to give them bread.

Joya called on his family each day. If I wasn't with one of his family, I would sit up on the roof of the house, reading, and praying. There was much to pray for in this beleaguered town. One morning, rapid footsteps came up the stairway to the roof. It was Joya, very troubled.

"Mum…please come. Our father is very sick…. could you pray for him?"

I quickly descended the stairs with him and entered their family room. His elderly father lay on a bed on the floor. The whole family had been called, and were gathered around him. He was pale, and in pain. He faded in and out of awareness. I asked Joya, could he explain to his father, who Jesus is? I wanted to ask the Lord to intervene, but not without his father knowing who it was I was praying to. He took a few minutes to explain Jesus to him, for the need for us to repent of our sin, to acknowledge that Jesus had died to satisfy God, and become God's true child. I asked his father, translated by Joya *"Do you understand?"* His father murmured he understood.

I then asked, through Joya's interpretation, could I lay my hand on his head? This for a Muslim man, is usually not allowed. But I was allowed. I prayed for the presence of Christ to minister to him. I asked the Lord, in His mercy, would He allow His healing virtue to flow through Joya's father's body. I prayed for a revelation of Christ to him. Joya said his father could feel something coming through his body. There was a strong sense of the presence of the Lord in the room.

I then left his family, to stay with him, as it was a deeply private family moment.

They considered he may be dying. They considered his chronic stomach disease had overcome him. He certainly seemed close to death. It was a perplexing hour for them. It was 3 days before Joya was to be married. Plans were feverishly being made for the happy event.

Less than an hour had passed, when I came downstairs, and was raising my camera to photograph the family's delightful courtyard garden. It was such a joyous distraction with the large melon vine arching over the lush green of the vegetables. A rose dangled to the right of the frame. But a figure appeared in the viewer of my camera. Dressed in a fresh white shalwar chemise, and the smartest waistcoat, and cap, was Joya's father! He walked with a strong gait and sweet glowing smile, towards me. There he was, totally risen from what had seemed a deathbed! I beckoned him to sit on the garden boundary in the foreground. I have that photo, of him in his pristine white outfit, squinting into the camera, fully healed! *Thank You Jesus!*

Each morning I climbed the stairs to the roof with my early morning cup of coffee for my bible time, with prayer for what might lay ahead in the day. Joya's father, like clockwork, would come up to the roof and check the level of the water tank. He needed to know daily, that there was sufficient water for the family's needs. After the presence of the Lord had come to him, healing him, he carried a beautiful smile.

The first morning after this, he placed his hand on his heart, and lifted his hands heavenward. It was a thanksgiving gesture to God. He then put out his hand for mine.

Each morning he did this, I would pray, in thanks, but also for a continuing acknowledgement of the Lord in his heart and mind and soul, and body. It became a precious ritual for the time I was with them. Each day he reached out his hand for me to take and pray. It seemed he loved being prayed for. It was a privilege for me, to serve him in such a small but eternally significant way.

He continued to go to the mosque. For the men of a village, the mosque is also the central place of information and daily news, not only a place of worship to Allah. I prayed that the Holy Spirit would hear him, and Father God, who he had not denied. His strength was maintained for the many weeks I was living with the family. He continued to be thankful to God, our God, and to Jesus whose ministry he had welcomed when lying so ill. He did not dismiss Him but was humble and thankful.

25.

CELEBRATION

The days were sunny in Autumn style, warm, but not oppressive. I was invited to go with Joya and his bride-to-be, on a shopping trip for their wedding rings, then to the bridal salon. I was allowed a view of the dress which was being hired for the wedding. The bridegroom first approves the outfit, then makes the payment. This was my first trip out into the streets. Apart from a walk to his bride Rahima's home in the next street, I had stayed in doors for five days, as a security. No Westerner is usually allowed to stay overnight in Hazaratown. I was to be with them for six weeks so I needed to be wise. I could not go for a walk by myself, but only accompanied.

In the fabric shop a blue sequined chiffon fabric was selected for my wedding *shalwar chemise* (long dress top with slacks) . This was to be made by the bride's sisters. It was being swiftly put together, and matched with a *dupatta* (head-covering) bordered with crocheted-lace worked by Joya's sister.

Come the morning of the wedding, the young women in Rahima's family, along with Joya's younger sister gathered in the bride's home. Spiced aromas came from the kitchen where her mother crouched on the floor, stirring the pots for a pre-wedding lunch. Joya's sister busied herself with painting in henna the most intricate, delicate patterns on hands and arms outstretched.

Rahima's sister worked on a sewing machine in another room completing my wedding outfit. Sweet giggles could be heard as necessary adjustments were made to the blue chiffon. I was much smaller than they had thought. Joya joined us with some Afghan music showing off his prowess in fine dance footwork to keep us entertained. He taught me where to put my feet and move with rhythm. I sat down out of breath.

Come afternoon, it was time to go to the beauty salon to be transformed for the all-important celebration. In Hazara culture, things do not go to a strict schedule. The wedding originally planned for 3.00pm was gradually shifted to 7.00pm. In a busy street in the marketplace, Rahima, her sisters, Joya's sisters and I, climbed the steps into a curtained sanctuary. The salon was a generous room of four-wall mirrors. Hairdryers and a vast array of cosmetic bottles were veiled in the mist and smell of shampoo and hairspray. The girls had their hair washed and shaped and sprayed. Their faces were made up and their nails painted. I decided to stay the way I was. I was already dressed in my completed blue chiffon with sequins My short haircut did not give a lot of scope for an exotic arrangement but the bride was being transformed.

The minutes passed into hours. The adjusted time for the wedding had long passed. The market was quiet, and it was dark outside. To wake myself up, I sprayed myself with sparkles. I had sat for so long, reason was fading. I had snapped endlessly on my camera, to capture their beautiful excitement. After all, it was why I had come. When the hours preparing the bride were finally completed, a phone call was made to let the bridegroom know, the bride was ready. Joya entered the salon dressed in smart, informal clothes, to dress half-way through the evening into his white bridegroom's shalwar chemise. It was embroidered by his bride, in the finest silk thread. He came with a bouquet for her of the richest red roses. A taxi was waiting. It was 9. o'clock.

To the beat of a Hazara drum, they made a dazzling entrance through the gates of the bride's home. Both wore garlands of roses given to them as they entered. Joya beckoned to me to enter the gates of the home with him. Young women danced ahead of us, to make a passage for the couple through the crowd. The courtyard was decked for the occasion. Wall lamps set a gentle and soft glow around faces. Beautiful Hazara faces, loved by God.

The men were in an adjacent room, having fed on wedding food, while waiting for the bridegroom to arrive. Fresh drinks were served to quench thirsts. It was a unique setting in a home, for these Afghan families. Weddings are usually held in vast public reception rooms and music amplified to many streets. Here, in the security of the bride's home, the beauty was in its simplicity. The Lord had given Joya the desire of his heart, to be with family and close friends, and at last to be a husband to his bride.

In a culture where the spouse is chosen for the couple, Joya and Rahima were given their love choice. It gave an exceptional element to their wedding, which their friends commented on. They said their love was like something from the movies. The first hours were taken for photographs with each family group until clapping began. It was time to dance. Afghan music was turned up as Joya entered the men's room dancing solo, firing up twenty of his companions, in twirling footwork.

In a quieter moment, in between dancing, Joya's cousin commented to him, that he had noticed that Joya had not entered in customary manner, with the Koran held over their head. Joya then shared with his cousin, that he was no longer a Muslim but a follower of Jesus. His cousin's face widened in a joyous smile.

"You are Christian! So am I!" It was a wedding gift to Joya, like no other. They hugged each other in particular understanding. His cousin was to be married the next week and vowed, he would take the same stand at his wedding. He too, would enter without the Koran. Both young men showed great courage. The Lord was with them, strengthening them.

We women guests inside the courtyard were eating our wedding supper and noisily chatting. A grand wedding cake carefully decorated with the bridal pair's names, waited to be cut, at the right moment. I sat in wonder that I was there among Afghan women, smiling and greeting me with such warmth. They were bringing their children and babies for me to hold, and have our photo taken. For me it was an exchange to be cherished. I recalled that moment in my home in Australia, six years before, asking the Lord:

"What do you want me to do now?"

"Women, casualties of war" ....

I marvelled at His fulfillment. I could never have arranged such a happening as that evening, of being encompassed by a cluster of them, holding their babies.

The music pulsed in the next room. The men were dancing and clapping in rhythm when the doors opened suddenly. One skilled dancer led Joya out into the courtyard to invite Rahima in a bridal dance. We clapped in hearty rhythm. Hazara gifts of flowers and medallions of prosperity were brought to them by the family and rings exchanged.

Guests were given gifts, until the time for the cake to be cut. The couple served a mouthful to each other as guests then queued for the same privilege. The bridal couple went to a private room to have their first meal together. What a night of joy and thanksgiving.

Back home in Australia, as little as six weeks before, Joya was impressed that he needed to go home for his family's sake, and to marry Rahima. We had prayed that if the Lord meant that to be, He would help us put it all together. Jesus was there at the wedding. His presence was so tangible. Hazara couples are traditionally expected to sit without smiling, but Joya's face radiated a beautiful peace and occasionally he chuckled with Rahima who broke into giggles behind her bouquet. The day after the wedding, her mother said:

"Nothing ever happens like that here, it was like a dream"

I think she reflected what many thought. There was something distinct in the wedding in its intimacy. The presence of the Lord gave it a dream quality.

According to custom, Joya and Rahima for the first week of their married life, received visits from extended family and friends, to congratulate them. His mother and sister worked busily to prepare sweet foods for each day of visits. These visitors were received in Joya's family home. There was a buzz of greetings, chatter and photos taken to capture the happy event.

The days settled, with opportunity to visit their friends and cousins, for even more eating of the wedding cake. With Joya and Rahima, and their mothers and sisters, with aunts and cousins, alot of cups of green tea were consumed, and plates of cake shared around. I was privileged to be included in these family moments. I wondered at the joy the Lord was giving me, being so accepted and encompassed in their favour. I could speak little of their language, but I was assisted in this by Joya translating.

We were yet to attend his cousin's wedding which was made distinct by the fact the bridegroom was a fellow believer.

Attending a Henna Night, before his cousin's wedding, we gathered in a grapevine-covered courtyard in the bride's home. Men and women were invited. Tempting dishes were brought from the kitchen to the tiny space, under coloured light globes hanging from the grape-vined ceiling. Above were the stars. The courtyard was packed with dancers to the beat of the Afghan stringed instrument called a Dumbora and drums. I simply sat and watched in wonder. In the hush of midnight, we walked home, talking softly. Stillness rested over the homes lining the dusty streets. A heavenly presence accompanied us.

26.

WATCHFUL

Also living with Joya's family here, was Mehdi, a cousin, who had lost both parents in Afghanistan. He worked away for seasons, but always returned to Joya's father and mother, who loved him as their own. He had made a special effort to be with Joya for his wedding. I woke up very early one morning, to find Joya's mother and sister, washing Mehdi's upper limbs. They were standing in pools of blood covering the floor and in the washtub. When I asked in shock what had happened, I was told he was target-shot at during the night while riding on his motorbike, on the outskirts of Hazaratown.

The intended bullet missed him but he came off his motor bike and suffered bloodied gashes to his hands. His arm was deeply lacerated. It brought the target-killing too close to home for this family. Wonderfully Mehdi's life was spared. I prayed for him, as I saw the family bathing his wounds. The blood loss was considerable. He was in deep shock.

In the days following at each opportunity, I spoke about Jesus to Mehdi, and prayed again for healing of the wound to his arm, praying also for a revelation to him of Jesus' love for him. He healed swiftly, which was a cause for great thanksgiving. He knew he had been touched by Jesus.

One night, while I was sleeping, there was a knock on my door. It was Mehdi, come to say good-bye. He was leaving in this early hour for Afghanistan, for more work. I said to him:

"You know Mehdi, you have been touched by Jesus".

He answered with a strong *"Yes"*.

I urged him:

"Follow Him Mehdi", and he nodded, tightening his grip on my hand. I prayed for him, to Father God, a Father to the fatherless. I asked the Lord to keep him safe, preserving him and fulfilling all that he has been created to be. He was 21 years old, and even in the dim light I could tell his face expressed a fresh hope.

Joya, in the days before his wedding, visited three separate friends, who had lost a family member in target killing, since he left for Australia. It is an ever-present reality for the Hazara Afghans. They live under a constant reproach from Sunni insurgents. I was in the Travel Agency, to book our domestic tickets to Islamabad, for our return trip home, when the travel agent handed me his mobile phone and said:

"Here is what it is like for us Hazaras". I screamed. There in the screen at gun point Hazaras were exiting a bus. As each one stepped out, they were shot dead. Twenty-eight all told, of fathers and young men, on their way to Iran to seek work, to support their families. This was boasted as the work of a Pakistan cell of Al-qaeda who posted the video.

One young widow with three children, whose husband died that day was brought to visit me, along with her widowed mother. They were seeking my help. I was intent, on representing her at the U.N. High Commission for Refugees. She needed a safe place for her three children to grow up. Her youngest babe was born after her husband was killed.

After some weeks of Joya and his wife enjoying married life, they with me, and his father, set off for Quetta City, to advocate for her, and for others seeking to be registered as refugees. Without this they have no status on which to apply for compassionate refuge in another country.

We took a local taxi for our journey, making our way along a rough dirt track to get out of the town, with the least possibility of being viewed. I was very mindful we were taking a risk. I studied every tuft of grass on that track, until we reached the Iran By-Pass which would take us into Quetta. The taxi was riddled with bullet holes. For certain, someone had died while travelling in it. The gunmen ride pillion and are ace shooters, coming alongside a car aiming with precision.

It was to be the first trip of a few we took to the city for the purpose of submitting applications for refugee status at the United Nations High Commission for Refugees.

The night after we made this trip, a message came from the mosque that two taxis had been gunned down. All occupants and the driver were killed.

A driver who took us on a subsequent trip, was to be applauded for his deftness. He held the taxi on the gravel verge of the road to the city driving at what Joya said was 100 miles an hour, on the left of the semi-trailers and trucks and other cars. This was to be out of the range of the shooters should they come. At moments on that journey I was tempted to cry out at our car tilting on the gravel verge at high speed, but kept my mouth shut. The driver was in intense concentration.

Earlier in the week, on the road just leaving Hazara Town, four Hazaras were killed in a roadside shop. A father, his two sons, and a worker did not go home that evening.

It sends a bleakness through the town and reminds the folk of the intentions of the Al-queda Sunni insurgents to eliminate them as Hazara Shi-ites. It has the effect of creating an anxious fear if a loved one is late. One evening Joya was delayed in a local government office where he had gone to register his marriage. It was dark and he hadn't come home. For the first time I began to dread that something had happened to him. This is what these families live with daily.

He woke me up early one morning, in tears. He had been by the graveside of a close school friend. In the evening before, he was alerted that his friend had been killed, as well as his father. Both had been shot dead in their shop in Quetta city.

According to Muslim tradition, the bodies have to be buried before sunrise the next day.

In the dark morning hours, Joya stood at the graveside and wept for his school buddy being buried. He was broken-hearted. As one travels up onto the Iran By-pass and looks back on Hazaratown, a whole hillside is sheathed in white posts, signifying the graves of those lost. From hilltop to valley below, all white. Hundreds of graves.

While we had taken that fast trip, travelling left of the trucks and lorries, on the gravel verge of the road, other drivers were less swift, though tensed to the wheel with eyes darting to the rear-vision mirror and back to the road. Seated in the front passenger seat I looked straight at a windscreen that had a bullet hole and radiating shattered glass. The safety belt hung slashed and frayed from its anchor. It was a chilling reference that one sitting in that same seat had had to be cut out of the taxi, dead. Joya's mother leaned over and placed her strong arms around me to keep me firm should we stop suddenly. She was keeping me from being thrown through the shattered windscreen.

Again came the news the day after, that a taxi with a family, had been gunned down along with the driver. In another instance, I was sitting in the back seat with Joya and Rahima, on our way to Quetta City, when we were caught in a traffic-jam. The taxi stopped dead, going nowhere. Joya took my hand, gripping it strongly. His face was white.

"This is very dangerous here Mum"

We were stuck in a Pashtun town of Sunnis who are at enmity with the Hazaras. A man on the curb fixed his gaze on me, frowning, apparent he had his eyes on a Westerner.

Kidnapping of Westerners is always a possibility.

"Turn away Mum, don't look at him, turn away" Joya urged me. I turned my head, and pulled my dupatta forward, shielding my face.

"From here to the bridge, the next two K's are really dangerous" Joya spoke fearfully.

Immediately into my mind came the promise of God's Hand shielding His children.

I simply said:

"Father Your Hand". We waited. Finally, the traffic moved out of the Pashtun village and along the treacherous kilometres to the bridge, without bullets. Our Heavenly Father shielded us.

Apart from the sadness and constant awareness of danger, the days were mellow.

I spent many hours up on the roof of the house. Their roofs are like open-air rooms surrounded by high walls. They are very private and out of view unless I stood at the wall and looked down on the life below me. Even while seated I could see out to the mountains turning from dusty pink as the day progressed into deep mauve as evening fell.

I spent many hours there, reading, and pondering, writing and praying. The opposite side of the valley consisted of the town of Mehra Bad, I had visited on my first trip with Kumiko.

On this side of the valley was Hazaratown. In total around 16,000 Afghans lived out their daily lives encompassed by sheltering mountains.

Each morning there was a sweet rhythm to the children setting off for school and workers riding their bike to work or walking to the township. As the morning progressed, the daily garbage collector came, and women made their way shopping, while the older men walked to the mosque. A few had the luxury of a motorbike. Next door was a sales yard for donkeys and chooks, and other livestock. The bray of the donkeys and roosters crowing, were a constant background, along with the sound of industrial workshops close-by. By evening children's play calls and kite-flying from rooftops made the sky-line a place of lively theatre. A blue sky, with dusty mauve mountains and the close of a warm Autumn day belied the fear they live with.

Amid the intense anxiety, families celebrate marriage, and babies are born, and families anticipate with excitement their toddler taking their first steps. It is little wonder with the constant reality of attacks on them as Hazaras, that when they celebrate they go crazy.

For family celebrations like Joya's cousin's wedding to which we were invited, Hazara songs are amplified at reckless decibels and dancing is furious and carefree. The women dressed in glitter on a scale that has to be seen to be believed. Old people sit and watch and remember. So much history is written on their faces.

His cousin's wedding lasted several hours of very intense amplified music from a public events venue. I needed refuge and found a spare room where I hoped I could rest. It was guarded by an elderly woman doorkeeper who allowed me to enter. However, when others sought to enter, she used a length of electricity cord to whip them back . When I looked alarmed at this, I had it explained to me, that the room was where the bridal couple sit to eat their first meal alone. The aged doorkeeper employed in this public venue, took her job very seriously, so used her whip with disconcerting success. As the room would not be needed for some time, she allowed me to stay, with the added gesture of bringing me a cup of tea. This privilege was given me as an older visitor to the wedding. I was humbled as well as revived, though troubled for those who had received her discipline.

At home with Joya's family, the afternoons continued to be a welcome time to chat with his younger brother, and when she could, his younger sister. I sat on a chair the family had brought out of storage, just for me. I was told it was a chair purchased for their great grandfather who lived until 105 years old. They both said they loved to come and talk with him, just like they were coming and talking with me. I viewed this as a great honour. In our chats I learnt a lot of the detail of their traditional beliefs.

The younger brother had a sharp intellect and a searching mind. They both were devout students of the Koran. We became buddies, comparing Koran with Scripture. In both I perceived a longing for righteousness. The younger sister, a beautiful young woman in heart and temperament, planned to travel to Iran to train as a teacher of the Koran to young women. The fact that she was prepared to take the treacherous journey reflected her deep devotion. She and I also enjoyed doing the household washing together. With lots of laughter, we untangled clothes as well as language.

I was not able to go out into the streets except for essential shopping. Standing at the wall of the roof, I daily looked out over the valley, and prayed: "*Lord, may Your kingdom come to this people.*" My thoughts regularly turned to Afghanistan across the border of the distant mountains. I prayed the same for the people in the land, that I had not yet seen. It was where the Lord had first focused my attention, believing, or simply hoping I would one day go.

There were many moments to pray, and I longed for Joya's family to know Jesus, for themselves. They were so respectful of my faith. Their Muslim sabbath was Friday, while in our tradition Sunday was when my thoughts went homeward to my church family worshiping. In an email home to them, one Sunday I wrote:

> 'Your day of worship is almost closing, and my thoughts
> are with you.

Here Sunday is just another day of bread-making and cups of green tea. Outside the sounds of a workday resonate; metal being cast and trucks and donkeys passing outside the front gate creating a storm of dust as they carry their loads. It is an industrial main road where the family lives here. But really it isn't just another day. There is cause for great celebration.

The Lord is faithfully answering your prayers for the family. Joya's bride gave her life to Christ last Thursday. He is deeply grateful to the Lord and comforted. He has been alone in his faith within the family for so long. Rahima's face is new. Thank you for praying for her'

Joya's mother wept one morning when I explained to her, that friends from home in Australia had given Joya the money for him and Rahima to go to Islamabad for a few days away just by themselves. I told her that our friends were happy they could help him come back to her and his father. In a quiet moment with her and me Joya explained the gospel to his mother. While she said she could not understand we prayed with her, that one day when she had learnt more about Jesus, she would be given a gift of faith.

She was deeply curious and appreciative. She said to Joya: *"Your God really loves you".*

With great joy, she took me to visit her close friend, a widow. I was feted with the finest sweet biscuits, nuts and dried fruits along with green tea. Sitting around her lounge room on cushions against the wall, with her daughters listening intently, she plied me with questions. I answered why I had come to Hazaratown, and who is in my family? She wanted me to come and stay with her, just like I was staying with Joya's mother. I explained, I was Joya's family's guest, and I would stay in their home for these weeks. Hazaras are intensely hospitable. Food and tea are their language of welcome.

Accompanied by Joya and Rahima, I went on a shopping trip to the village, to gather some gifts for friends and family when the time came to return to Australia. Bangles and fine fabric were my choice. Each shopkeeper was eager to know where I was from, and why come to Hazaratown?. They were intrigued to learn that Joya lived with me in my home in Australia and looked on him wistfully. To be far away from the terror of their hometown and living in a peaceful land seemed to be from a dream.

27.

EXILE

As the days passed, in a letter home to my friends praying for us I wrote:

> 'The days and nights here fold in together with a gentle rhythm. Unlike the nights in Quetta city last year, with repeated gunfire, and army trucks rolling by, the streets at night here have a velvet stillness of dimly lit doorways in small brick cottages. The one exception to stillness is the street-crier who sends out a shrill whistle on the hour to say, "all is well". I was walking home from Rahima's house close to midnight last week, with Joya's sisters when out of the shadow of an adjacent laneway, stepped a dark male form. He let out a scream of a whistle, frightening the daylights out of me. The girls laughed. He probably did too when he saw me jump. To this street crier I was obviously an identifiable novice in Pakistan.

This has been a different week this week for me, doing battle with a stomach bug, the kiss of Pakistan. I have withdrawn from regular meals and outings, which in some measure has been a blessing. It has given me extra time to contemplate and read the Word. On the rooftop in the late Autumn warmth, washing flapping in the breeze with the sounds of chooks and donkeys in the animal sales yard next door, it is an absolute luxury simply to sit and listen. I guess some of you would love to do that too. With family and work demands it is hardly easy is it?

Joya and Rahima returned from Islamabad yesterday and look utterly content to be married. They had a really enjoyable time exploring Islamabad and were welcomed home with great joy. In their absence I had more times to be alongside Joya's mother and his older sister. They now let me peel an apple for them, rather than insisting they peel an apple for me, as their guest. I am free to help them clear the tablecloth of dishes, which means they regard me as 'family'. In a culture observing a strict code towards a guest, these small allowances speak of their grace to me in their home. Yesterday I studied my Hazarigi grammar, while Joya's mother sewed on her manual sewing machine.

If you wonder at the lack of street photos, it is because I spend most hours watching the women cook in their unique Afghan pressure cooker and pans, or sit with them while they do the most exquisite embroidery and fine lace crochet. The latter is often worked in half-light because the power is off. The other hours I sit up on the rooftop looking out on the town and dusty mountains changing colour with the light. It is a rich exile.

As ever, thank you for your prayer for Joya and Rahima and everyone here. It wouldn't be as sweet a time without it, I am certain'

The Festival of Eid was approaching. It is an important celebration among Muslim believers. One is reminded of our Christmas, in the amount of cooking and planning and anticipation of family get-togethers. Every carpet was removed and shaken, and every windowsill and window wiped clean. Clothing is renewed, washed and ironed. Eid preparation brought a sparkle to everything. According to their tradition, it is a celebration of thanksgiving in the provision to Abraham, of a ram to be sacrificed, rather than Ishmael, as they believe. One longs for them to know the spotless Lamb, in Jesus, who was sacrificed and who rose in triumphant victory for them.

I appreciated their preparation out of devotion and affection for their fellow-Muslim neighbours and relatives. Many people made their way to friends and relatives, some holding brightly coloured gifts on their heads. As we made our way through the laneways to our planned invitations, we passed others doing the same. Greetings of 'Salaam' were exchanged. Joya's mother had prepared new clothes as gifts for the children of the friends we visited. Fine food was shared and lots of eager chatter. The Afghan pressure-cooker was brought out. Joya's mother and sister prepared a casserole of lamb and vegetables, seasoned perfectly with herbs from their roof-top garden. The Eid meal was delicious and the joy of the family so playful.

One evening late in Eid, Joya took me for a walk through the busy bazaar. In half-light festoons and shop windows sparkled. We strolled right across to the other side of Hazara bazaar, to a milk-shake shop, or rather, a Juice Shop as they call it. The mood was still celebratory with kite-flying for the children and families dressed in their best. We watched the stone-throwing competition which the men of the town take part in everyday! It is an ancient pastime.

28.

PLEADING

Our concern for those seeking to be registered with the United Nations High Commission for Refugees continued. It took persistence as every discouragement presented itself. The building in Quetta city which houses their office, is surrounded by bomb resistant walls of many concrete blocks padded and secured with sharp wire. For an hour we stood packed against others in the confined space between these wired walls before the office opened.

It required making our way through a door and down steeply descending steps worthy of a vault, into a small office space. We were met by a dismissive officer. Someone in another room heard my Australian voice becoming adamant, and calmly appeared to ask what I was wanting. He was sympathetic and spoke fluent English. He was reassuring and affirming in what I was trying to do for the families I was representing. He needed further documentation which we committed to submit in the following days.

The night before, Joya and his family and I had all joined hands while he prayed to the Lord for mercy for his family and acquaintances who had pleaded for help. Whether the U.N.H.C.R. would be the means of God's mercy we did not know. We were asking for His protective love for them, wherever they were, and whatever the outcome of our petition.

Acceptance by the calm, English speaking officer, of our initial submission was an answer to at least be heard. We were hopeful.

For this trip to the city, I was also intent on calling into the Christian Hospital, hoping to speak with the Medical Director concerning the plans laid for the Autistic Diagnostic and Development Centre. For months there had been no indication as to its development. As we entered the grounds of the hospital, there was a noticeable barrenness. Not one person was in the yard, where once families would be congregated. Warm greetings would have been made by a nurse at the front reception desk. As we came through the main doorway into the front foyer, all was empty. There was not one person there or in the corridors as we walked further.

A security buzzer had to be pressed to ask for entry into the administration offices. It was such a different place, which once would have been buzzing with life, a place full of people and greetings. Simply desolate. Joya and I were given permission to enter the administration section when they recognised my voice and name over the intercom. I asked could I see the Medical Director. He welcomed me warmly but as our greetings were made and the customary green tea called for, I could see he was reluctant for the subject of the Autistic Centre to be introduced.

"Our Diocesan Bishop could not give his blessing to our plans."

I recalled the months I had consulted with professionals in the field back home as well as the detailed research my companion and I had pursued. All this in insecure locations, as well as the time invested by the professional builder in designing and costing, it was a painful acceptance. They had been short-listed for an Australian Aid Grant. It was a deep loss of face for the Medical Director, particularly as it was he who had been eager for our help. I suggested that School and Home Support by professionals may be more realistic. I suggested these may be recruited through Mission organisations, but he explained he was overwhelmed with the present situation, when even to keep skilled doctors and nurses was difficult. Morale was low and compliance with the security police for their safety was a constant and wearying call.

The Doctors Without Borders had withdrawn all their workers, as had the Red Cross. All had been removed from the province of Baluchistan since the kidnapping and killing of the Red Cross Director. The essential Amputee Clinic had been closed. It was a sober time as we sat contemplating the grief that terrorist attacks had brought to the city. In the once thriving hospital, valuable support services now no longer existed. He explained how many medical specialists had left Quetta given the number of kidnappings and ransoms extorted.

The extraordinary protection of Father God has meant the hospital has never been a direct target of terror. This is a remarkable fact as it is situated right in the busy township on Mission Road, where individuals have been killed but never has anyone entered the gates of the hospital and brought destruction. May it always be so. Joya called for a taxi and we made our journey home.

Back in Hazaratown news of killings were shared from the mosque, or carried by personal messages to the families. Days of reports told of more sad news of a loved one somewhere in the town. The night after this venture into the city, news came that two taxis and their occupants had been riddled with bullets that day. It sent a chill through us, knowing that that could have been us, just one day earlier. We needed to ask the Lord when it was wise to travel.

Joya and I spent some hours over several days relating to families deeply suffering and needing help. Some had endured such heartbreak of multiple loss of loved ones. Once more we took the informal road up to join the Iran By-pass. I again studied every tuft of grass on that entry, praying for the protective Hand of our heavenly Father. Once on the highway the driver accelerated, and we were off.

Having lodged the papers with the UNHCR office, we planned to find somewhere to enjoy a meal, when Joya's phone rang. It was Kumiko, our Japanese missionary friend.

On hearing that we were in the city she was overjoyed. She expressed the desire to take us out for lunch to celebrate Joya and Rahima's marriage, so we made plans to meet up at a popular restaurant. It was a joyous re-union. Kumiko had not seen the family for a considerable time. The roads to Hazaratown had become too hazardous for her to make visits possible. The family love Kumiko, as many do, as she had nursed family members and cared for their medical well-being over years. After lunch, we retreated to Kumiko's home for a cup of tea.

While they were chatting, I decided to take a stroll through the garden surrounding the house where I had stayed the year before, first with my companion, and then the solitary weeks lying in bed at night counting the gunfire. Walking through the garden and orchard I gave God thanks for bringing me back yet again to Quetta, albeit in very different circumstances. It was not the same city. Constant kidnappings and killings had brought a wearying alertness and vigilance. So many workers had left. One couple from Costa Rica were still faithfully serving in the hospital, she a nuclear medicine doctor, and her husband a teacher in a local school.

A distinct pleasure that afternoon was walking out of the hospital gates and into Mission Road. It was a road I had walked down daily to shop for naan bread, groceries and fresh vegetables. and been welcomed with a cup of chai more than once. This time I walked with Joya beside me keeping guard. I went with purpose to meet up again with the two brothers in the sewing machine shop in whose home the previous year I had enjoyed an Eid meal. Their faces lit up when they saw me and received the small gifts I had for their mother and sisters. I introduced them to Joya who greeted them warmly. They chatted in Urdu.

Because of his joyous smile, they sensed he also was a Christian, and one asked him in Urdu:

"*Why are Christians so loving?*"

It was a deep and probing comment. It reflected what they and their family had perceived in the treatment of their father, by Dr. Pont, in the Christian Hospital. Joya translated all this to me as we went on our way. I asked him:

"*And what did you say?*"

Joya answered his question with speaking the words in Urdu:

"For God so loved the world that He gave His only begotten Son, that whoever believes in Him, shall not perish but have everlasting life". "Because God is loving". It was an unexpected delight to have had that conversation. The two brothers were doubly excited that they were both getting married the next Saturday, and would Joya and his wife and I come? They promised to send a taxi for us to take us to the wedding.

Having said good-bye to them, we continued our way down Mission Road and waved a rickshaw to take us to Jinnah Road. I needed to go to the Bank. The rickshaw dropped us in a side street. As we turned the corner and approached the bank, there on the footpath was a pool of fresh blood. We looked at each other and stepped over it. There was a crowd of men grimly frozen in stance and glare at me. as I made my way up the steps.

Someone had been shot in the last little while as the blood had not yet congealed on the warm footpath. I completed my bank transaction swiftly and we caught a rickshaw back to Kumiko's where the women were deep in conversation.

There was great reason for thanksgiving. It was a comfort for Kumiko and for us to be together. Her final visa to stay in Pakistan was fast running out. When she was a young nurse, newly arrived in Pakistan, she nursed Afghan refugees from the Russian invasion and had seen thousands fleeing the more recent rule of the Taliban. Joya's family were among the most precious and enduring of friendships. Her prayers and love for them, surely was why I was now able to live in their home, so easily and be received. The ground had been prepared over years by her and others in the Christian Hospital. It was Kumiko who two years before had driven me out to their refugee town. She knew the treatment the Hazaras received in this city, and the attempts constantly made by the Sunni insurgents to eliminate them. She had always nursed them with such professional care, just as she did all those who came to the hospital, whatever their faith tradition.

We gathered our things to leave. I was wearing the traditional navy and white full-length street covering of the Hazara women. I still had not mastered the art of securing it firmly over my head, under my chin, tossing it over my left shoulder and securing it with a pin.

Joya's mother lovingly arranged it for me. It was a tender gesture. When completed, Kumiko said:

"Marion now a Hazara".

In the next five weeks Kumiko would be packing her belongings and leaving after serving in the land for 30 years. We hugged each other and spoke our final goodbyes at the compound gate. The taxi had arrived to take us home. I looked back. Kumiko stood with dignity and waved a soft wistful farewell.

29.

CLOSING

The days with my Hazara family were swiftly closing. In a final email to family and friends praying for us back home I wrote:

'You have faithfully read these news updates and stood with us, and for us, before Father God, and we are very grateful. I do not take that for granted, and pray for you too that you will know the presence of the Lord, forwhatever situation you are in right now.

This week I broke! Pakistan always breaks me! I always reach a point where I am reminded that it is only by God's grace.

Thursday night, Friday, through to Sunday I was fighting a wretched flu virus which has attacked a lot of people around the town, and it took every ounce of strength. The confines here, while listening to frequent sad news, overwhelmed me. With a call to home, and a couple of emails to let some of you know, the response brought a strengthening from the Lord, as you prayed for me. Thank you! Joya also very wearied has managed to fight it, though the virus has been hanging around him. He has been pressing on.

He so perseveres and loves making us laugh with his antics to jolly us all along when we get too serious.

Wonderfully I was in full health by last Monday morning to go with Joya and his Dad, and Rahima into the UNHCR to submit further documents that they requested. We were given a good reception. When I said: "Thank you, I am very grateful" the officer saluted me. I was surprised as well as blessed.

We celebrated afterwards with a hearty meal. The rose garden surrounding the restaurant provided a welcome retreat for wandering. I found it renewing after being unwell. Joya's father was all smiles. His face is new. We were very thankful we were kept on the hazardous road. It is not an easy journey.

We had planned to return to UNHCR office today for others, but last night heard that two *passengers and a taxi driver were killed by gunmen on that same route that we had taken the day before. We will only return as we sense the protective power of Christ. He will determine outcomes, as we stay in His purposes. The wedding in Quetta on Saturday was not on our agenda as no taxi arrived as promised. We presume the family did not consider it wise. I was laid low, so it wouldn't have been possible.*

There is a lot to give God thanks for, albeit in the midst of uncertainty and weariness. Last week and this week, hours have been filled with exchanges with those in need and preparing submissions for them. Joya and I have needed patience where rounds of discussion with extended family and friends had to be managed with great care. Where people are broken and desperate Jesus wants them primarily to know they are loved. As Joya and I have prayed for grace and wisdom, the Lord has done some gentling in situations that were potentially conflict-bound. Thank You Father!

While all this has filled our days, in the evening now, I am sitting with the family in their family room, the younger ones are reading, and the two women doing their embroidery and crochet. We have lots to talk about after dinner in the evenings, and with interpretation from Joya's younger brother, I am able to take part. We leave Quetta as planned, on Sunday, then fly out of Islamabad Monday, arriving Sydney on Tuesday...."

It was a tearful hour as the family gathered for our goodbyes. Joya's father and I hugged each other, as I prayed for him and his family. Only Jesus could have created that moment. A cultural Muslim man would not normally touch a woman, let alone allow a mutual hug. There were tears in his eyes and mine. Father God had done such a work in his heart and mind and soul. He had also healed his physical body. Joya's mother and a close friend, with his younger sister, Joya and Rahima and I climbed into two waiting taxis to travel to the airport.

No words of comfort were sufficient for the newly-weds. Joya and I stood on the steps of the airport terminal and looked back. He was holding back tears. I said:

"Go back and hold her again, there is time".

He fast footed it back into the carpark to the taxi where Rahima and his mother were sitting. I found it hard to say goodbye. This family had loved me as their own.

On our return to my home in Australia, we learnt with alarm that the night after we flew out, two taxis taking families to the airport, for the identically timed flight as ours had been gunned down on that small road entering the airport carpark. In the six weeks we had spent in Hazaratown, and for three days following, we learnt that 39 people had lost their lives by target shots. Most were killed on the road where God had kept us for four return trips. Eight treacherous journeys.

To date, no Westerner had been allowed to stay overnight in Hazaratown. God had determined in His mercy for me to stay 42 days and nights, in safety. His love had protected us for His kingdom purposes. It was a sober privilege. I longed to return and in the following weeks after arriving home, made application to the Pakistan Consulate in Sydney, to go in the following year as a visitor. I wanted to rent a tiny house and tutor English for heavenly purposes. Perhaps not surprisingly that application was refused as I was not going with a Non-Government Organisation, but simply on a personal application.

Had I flown out on the ticket I had booked for this intended journey, I would have come to Hazaratown in crisis.

On the date of my planned arrival a tractor hauled a water tank, down the informal track from the Iran By-pass. It passed by Joya's family home. It had 800 kilograms of explosives hidden. It was remotely detonated and 112 Hazaras were killed in the shopping centre. Had it been detonated 3 minutes earlier, both Joya's and Rahima's family would have been killed. By then, Joya was living interstate from me and rang me in anguish.

"Mum, it is terrible. Many killed. The shop where you bought the bangles? All gone. Whole end of bazaar is gone.!" He was in shock.

Rahima called me and begged me to get her out of there. There was little I could do, except pray. I ached to be with them.

PART 4
2013

30.

UNFULFILLED

While my heart and mind were daily engaged in the lives of those I had lived with or related to in Pakistan, I still wondered about the strong word concerning the land of Afghanistan that I had received so many years before. I had taught Afghan women in my own city and visited them in their homes over a season of two years. I had taught others in Islamabad, and had the deep privilege of living with my Afghan family in Hazaratown on the outskirts of Quetta in Western Pakistan. As yet I had never been in their homeland.

The organisation I had gone with to Pakistan had no work in Afghanistan, so I made enquiries with another organisation. It required being trained by them and submitting to scrutiny as to my suitability. I underwent psychological testing for temperament and resilience. So far, so good. One remaining question was regarding my physical strength or vulnerability. I was hardly a youthful applicant.

It was understandable that this should be brought into question. When I was leaving Hazaratown, a woman who had received much comfort in a critical condition wanted to hug me in farewell. There was a strange fierce gratitude at my leaving as she threw her arms around me. Her strong hands hit my spine. She persisted to press strongly gripped hands against my vertebrae and I begged her to let me go. The pain was excruciating.

With help from another she finally let go. I had to lie down to recover from the shock. After resting, I recovered with only moderate discomfort remaining in my back.

Three months after returning home to Australia, my vertebrae finally snapped. Scans and X-rays revealed I had sustained a progressive fracture, from the strong hold I had received. Knowing her history of suffering and the rage still lodged in her soul, made it a simple thing to forgive her. I thought long and hard about her and wondered how she was.

As a young mother in Afghanistan her husband, had been killed to settle a family blood feud involving his brothers. Custom dictated that the dead husband's parents then became legal guardians of their two children. She, the widow had to leave. She was no longer wanted. It is a cruel custom, and one I have heard from another Afghan widow who was put out on the street when her husband died.

This particular one, who hugged me, had returned to her biological family, now living as refugees in Hazaratown, Pakistan. A new husband was found for her. As a fruit seller, he travelled each morning on the Iran By-Pass to the markets to buy his fruit to stock his barrow for the day. One day he did not return. He was one of many shot that day on that hazardous road. Again she was widowed, while her heart ached for her children living far away in Afghanistan.

While I was in Hazaratown, she came to the home where I was staying. I was asked by Joya would I please pray for her? He took me to the room where she was lying on a mattress on the floor. She rolled about wailing. I knelt down beside her, and gently turned her shoulders towards me. I was shocked to see the terrible bruises on her face, and injured eye. The side of her face was swollen, and the injured eye barely open. Red welts were risen around her neck. I sat her up and cradled her. She whimpered and sobbed in my arms.

It was difficult to hold back my own tears. I bleated to Jesus to comfort her, to heal her. I already knew the history of the loss of her children. It was sufficient grief in itself, but now to see her so battered was almost too much to bear. She had married a third husband and they lived with the husband's adult son and wife. Her adult step-son had vented his hatred of her coming into fill the place of his mother. This battered young woman was hardly into her thirties. She fell into a calm, untroubled sleep as I laid her back on her mattress.

I saw her face healed in a few days, and a smile which radiated a brilliance and fresh hope. Joya persuaded her husband to find a separate home to rent, well out of range of the step-son's anger. When she learnt I was leaving to return to Australia, she came to say goodbye. It was then with a soft look in her face she reached out her arms to hug me fondly. As I held her in that embrace, it was then the incongruous gesture perhaps in fervour rather than intending to hurt me.

Now back in Australia, I needed strong two hourly painkillers and daily rest to heal.

One morning on waking I realised I was pain-free for the first time in eleven weeks. My back felt like silk. I was healed.

This medical history was an issue with the organisation, when I applied to go into Afghanistan. I assured them I was prepared to take the risk, and persisted in hope I was able go. After a lot of deliberating, considering the risk, they finally gave me the go-ahead, but only for a month to see if I could manage. Seven months after applying I paid for my ticket and prepared to go. I was to work with a Non-Government Organisation concerned with the re-building of Afghanistan after years of war. I was recruited to teach English in a Women's College which had been established.

On the day my church family gathered around me, and my Pastor prayed for me before leaving, it was 7 years from the exact date that I had received the word from the Lord:

"*Women…casualties of war………Afghanistan*"

In faith believing I would be able to go, I had made myself a long black dress-coat to wear.

In a number of Islamic cultures a 'widow' as I was considered usually wears black. It would save any cautioning comments to be known as a widow. I was not simply an older woman alone. There was a particular joy as close friends waved me off with tears at the departures door at the airport. At last!

31.

ANTICIPATION

The descent into Kabul, the capital of Afghanistan was a moment to be cherished. We had left Dubai and flown at 26,000 feet across the Arabian Sea, of pristine blue. The captain explained each turn in the aircraft for us to fully appreciate the route we were taking. The Arabian Sea was so clear one could see the mountains submerged in the depths. Flying straight ahead, across the escarpments of southern Iran, and turning right over the rural landscape of southwest Pakistan, the plane headed north. It seemed with pleasure the captain explained we would then turn gentle left and cross the Hindu Kush mountains into Afghanistan. Encircling the snow-covered peaks one could see the precarious roads by which so many must have travelled to escape conflict. The descent was gentle into the land I had waited to see.

I accepted the first offer of help with my luggage at the exit door of Kabul airport. But after going through a time-consuming police check point out into the public area, discovered the helper had misunderstood me. I needed the domestic airport in order to fly to the north.

I was heading for the city of Mazar-e-Sharif. So back we went on the long walk to the check-point and the queue waiting again to be checked. It helped reduce my waiting time which was filled with making friends with an Afghan family heading the same way. I was almost to my long-anticipated destination. As we ascended in flight to the north, the city of Kabul was jewelled in dusk.

I was so grateful for assistance with my luggage from two young Afghan men on arrival in Mazar-e-Sharif. They were careful to see me safely collected by my host and committed to wait with me until he had arrived. When all the travellers were met and every hopeful taxi driver left, still no host arrived for me. The young men were concerned so lent me their mobile to ring my host, asking:

"Where are you?". It seemed the arrival time had been confused. With the two young men having to go on their way, I was the only person left standing under a fierce check-point light in the middle of a vast acreage of otherwise empty land.

I glanced over at an army tent close-by where five Afghan soldiers were huddled around a fire burning in a hole in the ground. They had their berets tightly pulled down over their ears, and black scarves covered their nose and mouth from the cold. All I could see were five pairs of dark eyes fixed intently on me. I smiled as an expression of peace and secured my woollen shawl over my head and tightly around my shoulders. The cold was biting.

I was standing close-by the armed soldier on duty under the most intense glare of the check-point light. The light was so bright I had to shield my eyes in order to see my luggage at my feet. I decided to leave my luggage there and take a slow walk out of the glare but keeping within the arc of light so they could still see me and not be troubled.

In the far distance I could see the lights of Mazar-e-Sharif. I looked up to a cloudless velvet sky with numberless stars in sequined expanse. Our Father God seemed so close.

"Father I'm here…" As if God didn't know.

I remembered asking Him:

"What do You want me to do now?"

I was standing in His answer.

I was grateful that my host had been given the wrong information on arrival time. It provided this moment to reflect on the faithful character of God in Christ, to teach me, prepare me and entrust me with this journey. My host finally did arrive with great apology, but it wasn't necessary. I had relished the wait and the moment.

32.

MAZAR-E-SHARIF

From the window of my second-storey room, in a suburban street in Mazar-e-Sharif, I looked out on my first early morning to workers making their way to the markets. Mothers were fully covered in blue burkas. These are a full-length gown, with a lattice weave over their face, out of which they can see, and speak. Their form and face are not visible. They were walking hand in hand with their children while a beggar in a wheelchair was hoping for his first coin. It was a quiet deep joy to see at last where I had for a long while imagined I might be. I was to be living for this month in the home of the Director of the Non-Government Organisation I would be working with. He and his wife and family welcomed me.

The first venture out into the streets came in the afternoon when I was taken to the Women's College to meet the teachers. We sat down to a traditional Afghan meal where I was plied with many questions from the teachers, and then from the students as

I was taken into the classes. It was planned for this month that each afternoon I would be tutoring the students in small groups, and assisting the Afghan teacher of English in any way she found helpful. In the mornings I would receive the benefit of a one-to-one lesson in the Afghan language of Dari. For these I would go to the International Assistance Mission headquarters about a kilometre from where I was staying.

The city of Mazar-e-Sharif goes at a measured pace, so unlike Quetta that I had come to experience. With laconic car horns and wide dusty streets, blue burka-clad women and girls wearing white head coverings were in constant view. Men in shalwar chemises, the baggy pants and long shirt, with the traditional hat of a rolled brim, walked or cycled. All moved in gentle motion. Sellers park their fruit barrows in the street, laden with apples and pomegranates, while others, some quite young, worked on building sites. As we travelled in the van to the College, I saw a substantial crowd of men at a major corner who I was told were waiting for work. We passed the famous Blue Mosque.

Because of the tight security in which foreign aid workers are kept, life settled into a daily routine of listening for the sound of the horn of the van waiting outside the gate to take me to wherever I needed to go. I was advised not to go out of the huge metal gate by myself but only to get into the van. It became a rigid ritual. An exception was made for when I needed to go to the local shops.

On these days Faisal the doorkeeper wheeled his bike as I walked alongside. He would then load my groceries onto his bike and accompany me home. I took my turn to cook the evening meal and learnt which was the best rice to purchase in the corner shop. Afghan rice is deliciously sweet. On the pavement outside the grocery shop was a freshly butchered sheep hanging waiting to be carved. Next to the young salesman was a live sheep waiting his turn.

On days when the van could not collect me, I enjoyed walking to my Dari lesson. I came to enjoy these leisurely accompanied strolls to the International Assistance Mission. Faisal strapped to his bike, my loaded backpack with Dari language books and lecture notes for tutoring later in the afternoon. These walks together gave me some moments to absorb the atmosphere of the streets.

One morning waiting for the van which was to come, I stood in the courtyard by the doorkeeper's little cabin in the wall when a metallic crack sliced the air and the ground shuddered under my feet .

"Faisal!" I shouted. *"Bomb!"*

The old gentleman he was, emerged from his cabin and with a sober look on his face simply murmured in agreement and slowly rocked his head in sorrow. We learnt later that a suicide bomber, just one block away had intended to kill a local government officer. Instead he killed three children simply walking to school, and himself.

My days of tutoring at the Women's College, introduced me to girls eager to learn.

They were in their late teens and early twenties. Some were in the later High School years of education, while others were at Teachers' College. Some were studying for degrees in particular disciplines. The College provided essential English literacy education supplementing what was already taught at their particular institutions. My aim in the month was to bring their reading and writing English to life, by speaking English. This as well as sharpening their spoken grammar.

As the days progressed, the tutorials offered opportunity for the students to tell their stories, and to question me on my life. Dramatic role-playing of their current English lesson in class provided some great interactive moments. They enjoyed my limited drawing skills to depict certain scenarios, so laughter became a regular response. It came to be fun.

The Afghan teacher whose class I was tutoring commented:

"Miss Marion, my students come back from your class always happy"

It was a sound encouragement as I opened each tutorial with prayer to our Father. I asked for His blessing on our time and help for them and me. I closed our tutorial in prayer also.

When introducing this to my students, I explained who I was praying to, and gave anyone who wanted to opt out while I prayed, the opportunity to do so. Among 30 students only one chose to opt out. The rest were happy with this routine.

It was of considerable value to be living with a family. The couple and three children lived in a comfortable three- level home with a generous garden space. They had lived 11 years in Afghanistan and were utterly familiar with the measured pace of this northern city. I marvelled at their ordered acceptance of life in Afghanistan. The parents departed for work and children left for school early, before I had time to eat my breakfast. I was ready by mid-morning to be picked up for my Dari Lesson. Dinner times in the evening provided space to discuss the day. Sitting with the children around the dinner table helped fill the void of being far away from my grandchildren.

Our weekly lunchtime fellowship in the College office, gave opportunity to study the Word, and pray for each other. These and Sunday nights with a shared meal and fellowship with others of our organisation were essential in a context of foreign worship. Another blessing was a bigger gathering of believers working with other organisations, which was held fortnightly in other homes. How precious to Father God must be the trust these families and singles place in His hands to stay in such a place of foreign culture. While on guard and cautious, respecting the laws of the land, they displayed great courage and calm.

With predictable regularity, the season of Muhurram returned. As I sat on the rooftop on the evening of the 10th day, a discordant hum rang out. Sunnis in thanksgiving, and Shiites in mourning. One could only beg for mercy from God, for each to know their true Deliverer. One email I had already sent home to those praying for me tells you more:

> *"I pray this finds you well and rejoicing. If you are not well, or struggling, I pray Father God truly meets you and ministers into your situation He is present with us and ever mindful of us isn't He? In love and mercy with power.*
>
> *Today, a Muslim Sabbath, I joined other brothers and sisters in a home fellowship. We listened to a Tim Keller teaching on John 15. It was good and gave rise to a lively discussion followed by a very personal and far-reaching prayer-time for each other. To listen to others and learn what ventures for Jesus are happening, is truly inspiring. There are those here who have persevered faithfully, some*

for many years, others for fewer. Some newly arrived are simply learning the language but all with some kind of struggle or another.

It is the season of Muhurram at present, the fourth now that I have been present for, when the Shia community acknowledge their particular suffering.

It is a vulnerable time for them when they are often freshly persecuted. A bomb was found in the Shia mosque down the street this week, before being detonated. Your prayers are deeply significant and powerful. Thank you for praying and continuing to pray for safety here. Next Thursday is the 10th day, when we cannot go out at all. Particular protection is needed for the surrounding neighbourhood on that day.

Our brothers and sisters need particular prayer for this season, as the oppression becomes tangible, more tangible than most times. A lot of wailing and special lengthy messages amplified from the mosques resonate through the streets and are very oppressive.

I had my first Dari lesson this week, a challenge but a good challenge. I go each day Saturday to Wednesday in the mornings then teach in the afternoons. I am doing tutorial teaching with a few students at a time for 35-40 minutes and enjoying it. I meet for lunch with National staff beforehand and test my simple Dari with them. Laughter is a great saver in this context and there are delightful opportunities in my tiny classes when we become tangled in language differences, to simply laugh.

When lessons close at 4.00 pm it is strange to see the students set off. Some are in black outfits, covering their faces with only eyes seen, while others don their bur-kas with no view of their face at all. One moment they are chatting giggling girls or young women, while in the next, incognito. I love seeing their faces as I teach, and we chat together, and when the moment is given, to pray.

I went for my first shopping trip yesterday and had the shock of having my money purse stolen from my shoulder bag. Some soul is now in the possession of US $60 I pray they are blessed by Jesus as it is His money. I asked Him could He give them a dream of Him, as He is giving many here.

How He loves with mercy.........Thank you for thinking of me. I love your emails.... In Him."

I came to look forward to my daily Dari vocabulary and grammar lessons. I had a formidable young Hazara Afghan man to teach me. We became good friends. He was in his final year of a Law degree. I shared some of what my life in Australia comprised, and that I had an Hazara "son" who had lived with me in my home in Sydney for many months.

I explained my time in his family home, in the refugee town, and how that taught me alot about Afghan culture and beliefs. I explained that I had many young sons and daughters in my faith family back home in Australia and quoted the promise in God's Word.

'More are the sons of the widow than she who is married'. While this has relevance in Isaiah's prophecy to Israel, it was of signifi-

cant comfort to me personally. My teacher's eyes filled with tears when I spoke from the Word. God gave us a sound trust of each other and he was free to express his anxieties with me concerning his approaching final year exams. Even though he was of a different faith tradition, I asked him would he appreciate me praying for him? He said yes, he would appreciate that. I prayed for him there and then. He was quiet and grateful.

I worked on my Dari vocabulary, verbs and grammar homework and began to freshly enjoy attempting to respond to him in my lesson time. When he taught me Afghan greetings I couldn't resist sharing one of ours in Aussie vernacular, cupping my hands around my mouth and sending out a resonant:

"Gooday mate!" He threw his head back laughing from his belly.

At the close of the lesson I waited in the International Assistance Mission headquarters' kitchen where it was warm. The chill coming off the distant snow- covered peaks surrounding the city was beginning to be felt. I hugged the wood-fired heater in the kitchen. These moments offered time to pause, and watch Jameel prepare dinner for the staff. The rich aroma of food bubbling on the stove and her welcoming smile were comforting. I loved those moments in her company as I waited for the van's horn in the lane, to take me to the Women's College. She and Isaac the gardener were touches of home for me.

Isaac tendered the headquarters' garden with zinnias then in final bloom before winter, and roses clinging to the garden wall. I explained to him in my limited Dari, that my *Padah* (father) also grew zinnias. He also loved Jesus. I said my *Padah* was now with Jesus, pointing to the heavens. He smiled a radiant knowing smile.

In the late afternoons, I would sit on the rooftop of where I was staying, just as I had done in Hazaratown. It was a time to ponder the day's activities. My chair on the rooftop was also a favourite place for the days when I did not teach. I had a view of life across the rooflines of neighbouring homes and below in the street. One glimpse was of men on the next-door roof, laying great slabs of fresh mud on the roof. I had it explained that before winter comes the roof is freshly laid to cover the existing mud roof which had dried out and cracked in the intense summer heat. The nights were becoming cold heralding a bitter winter. I rugged up for my evening reflections on the rooftop.

Looking out over to the opposite side of the street, I could see people coming and going from the police station. Women in blue burkas or fully black, sat on a simple wooden form on the pavement waiting for their turn to be seen. It is an established fact that many Afghan women suffer domestic violence and poverty. Many struggle with addiction.

On one of my shopping ventures, a rough gnarled soiled hand reached out of a burka and a woman's voice begging. I put some Afghan notes into her hand, gifts from my brothers and sisters back home. I closed her palms around the notes and held her closed hand with my own firmly. "*Issa* (Jesus)" I repeated His name and prayed for her to have a revelation of Him. I wanted her to know it was Jesus who loved her and cared about her.

She nodded. I held her in a hug for a significant moment as our heads lent against each other. One's heart pleads for such a one, possibly an opium addict given the state of her dirty hands and burka, or simply homeless, perhaps a widow cast out.

On our van trips to the city, we passed the Women's Prison. It is a fact that some women will be there for their whole life, for having murdered their husband. Some husbands have been so cruel to their wife or daughters that the woman takes revenge. Some have sought justice for domestic abuse and are themselves gaoled or young ones run away from an arranged marriage and are arrested and gaoled. Some are imprisoned for assault, theft or narcotics charges. Women are there in their young life, for so-called moral crimes having conceived a child out of wedlock. For five years they are incarcerated unless a judge modifies the sentence. There are two categories of law, Jurga and Civil.

Depending on which is referred to in judgement sentences can vary. Great variation also exists in the legal outcomes depending on the province. As a rule, the young pregnant mother is gaoled and gives birth while serving her sentence. Her child lives with her.

Working for a Non-Government Organisation a young woman, a foreign aid worker, has established a Pre-School in the prison in Mazar-e-Sharif. It is staffed by trained local Afghan women. She has also given the young mothers opportunity to become literate in their own language. It is a noble venture and has brought great joy to the children and comfort to the mothers. When I inquired about opportunity for the older women to develop, at that time no foreign aid personnel was working with them. I kept that fact stored in my heart.

As well as establishing the Pre-School the same young woman teaches English in a boys' orphanage. I had the experience of travelling some kilometres out into the countryside, with her. What a committed servant. The boisterous boys love her. She turns up daily in consistent determination to love and teach them. I admired her courage and perseverance. The boys have either lost both parents, or their mothers have been widowed and unable to keep them. Yet another outcome of continuing conflict in Afghanistan.

While sadness easily came for the people of Afghanistan, there were times of rich fellowship. To quote from an email I sent home:

> *"Tomorrow brothers and sisters from the expat community meet for a fortnightly gathering. I look forward to these. They are so unique in a foreign context. Earlier this week one evening in a small sitting room, a visitor led an evening of worship with her keyboard. The presence of the Lord came so comfortingly and reassuringly, our songs drowning out the wails from the mosque down the street. We had communion together and prayed for this land and its people......*
> *May you know how much your prayer companionship means to me, but also to brothers and sisters with whom I fellowship.'*

Comfort also came in the presence of others from the local community who loved Jesus.

The housekeeper where I was staying was such a one. As a widow left with six children, she had a dream of Jesus and enquired about Him. She came to a resilient trust of Him, and it showed. While illiterate she had the scriptures orally taught to her. Her eldest daughter was in one of my English tutorial groups and her manner reflected a sound faith.

On each Muslim Sabbath the family sing worship songs to Jesus in their mother tongue while her literate daughter reads the scriptures to them. Their mother delighted in my stumbling Dari and often simply smiled and hugged me. She lovingly accommodated my clumsy search for words.

In the latter weeks of my month's stay, the local Afghan English teacher who I was supporting, had to go for a university interview. She was hoping to gain entrance to study for a degree. She asked me would I take her classes in her absence. I was delighted. I had got to know the students in our small group tutorials and it offered an opportunity for them to know in more detail my life in Australia. I asked the Director of our Organisation was I free to explain my faith, without jeopardising the work of the College? He gave me the freedom to do so.

Two classes of 15 students listened eagerly as to what my family comprised, what I had studied, and why I wanted to come to Afghanistan to teach English. In one class the moment came to share my testimony of coming to faith in Christ. Complying with the principles of the land I had no intention of persuading but simply to explain. I told them the moment came when I needed to say sorry to God for my life. I lived without Him. I thought I was a good person, but God is Holy. I needed to say sorry to Him for turning away from Him. I believe God's Son, Jesus took my place before God when He died for my wrong.

God forgave me, and Jesus made a home in my heart: '*Honay Issa*' a 'Jesus home' placing my hand on my heart.

In the class where I shared this detail, a murmur began among the students. One student turned to another. The only mature-aged student in the back of the class puzzled and asked of her classmates: "*Honay Issa?*" The other students said to her, pointing to their heart, each in turn explaining: "*Jesus home*". The phrase was echoed through the class.

At the end of the lesson one of the students, a more competent speaker of English, came to me and told me, the older student who puzzled over my comment, wanted to invite me to her home for a cup of tea. With interpretation I made a day when I could respond. Her home was easy to find, as she lived in the same street as the College. I was welcomed eagerly by her and her married daughter who could speak functional English.

We sat down on the floor in traditional style for our cup of tea. Her daughter explained to me, that her mother was very interested:

"You talked in class of 'Honay Issa' "pointing to her heart. *"She wants you to tell her how?"*

This I did, explaining the gospel to her, while her daughter interpreted.

I had in my backpack one copy of a Dari New Testament. I opened it to the first chapter of the gospel of John and invited the daughter to read it aloud.

'This is who Jesus is" I explained.

As she read the daughter's face changed in eager wonder. She excitedly explained to her mother what she had just read, enlarging on the meaning. Her mother murmured in interest, leaning eagerly towards the Testament in her daughter's hands. They were excited and the daughter hurriedly read more aloud.

The mother explained that she had an uncle in Germany who believed in Jesus. She was so grateful to me to come and explain what it was he believed. Now she understood. I suggested they could keep the New Testament, so they could read more. Both were grateful. They allowed me to pray for them to grow in their search.

I enquired then about my student's husband who was lying ill on a mattress on the floor, coughing and gasping for breath. They and he allowed me then to pray for him for Jesus to give him breath, laying my hands on him, that He might be healed. I prayed also for a revelation of God in Christ for him. He fell asleep and slept peacefully as we sipped our tea and talked about family. Time was quickly passing. I needed to walk back to the College to be driven home.

As we strolled to their front gate for farewells, her husband, who had woken up called out to me in Dari. He was walking towards the gate to join us. The daughter laughed, and said:

"*My father says you must stay, you must come to live in our home*".

I shook his hand, and said:

"*Tashakor*" (Thank you) I understood his invitation was in gratitude for being given fresh breath and a healing sleep. His cough had ceased. *Thank You Jesus!*

Another cup of tea with pleasure was shared with a university student I had assisted with some English conversation. We walked together one afternoon through the streets of Mazar-e-Sharif and up a lane to her home. In these wide dusty streets there were no trees or grass, and certainly no footpaths. Rubbish and pools of mud had to be navigated before arriving at the gate where we knocked and waited.

Typically a mother, if not a widow out working, spends her days at home, as in this case.

She and her husband had encouraged their daughters to become educated, out-witting the expectations of traditional cultural standards. This particular daughter who brought me to her home was progressing well through a Medical degree, with promise of a valuable career.

One of the teachers at the Women's College who was well into studying for a university degree, was majoring in English Literature. She asked me for assistance in one of her assignments, which was a joy. She was the youngest of five children. Her mother had been a teacher. During the Taliban rule, only chants of the Koran in Arabic were considered appropriate and that only for the boys. Education for girls was totally banned. Not to be defeated their mother would go secretly to the marketplace where contraband textbooks and literature on all subjects were collected. All through those years she home-schooled her five children with excellent results. This particular daughter, had four brothers who all were now practising either engineering or law. A triumphant mother indeed, of whom her children were proud.

As my time in Mazar-e-Sharif was closing, a feast was held for Thanksgiving Day. There were a number of American N.G.O. workers for whom this was a not-to-be-missed tradition. It was held in my hosts' home large enough to accommodate many adults and a backyard bustling with children playing. It was a happy day where some had travelled many kilometres from outlying towns to take part.

Before enjoying a banquet of food, we all sat around on cushions on the floor, and opened our time together with a prayer to honour our heavenly Father as the giver of all good gifts. We were invited to individually speak out what we particularly wanted to thank God for.

One young father of four children spoke about the past year as one of extreme challenge.

So great had been the spiritual contest of their work in a remote town that he had been crushed and despaired of its purpose. He wanted to give the Lord thanks for his wife who had encouraged him at his darkest times not to give up. He spoke of the fresh courage that the Lord had given him, because of her faith for him. He said he would not have made it without her. A beautiful word and one I still recall clearly.

It was a particular joy that I was at the International Assistance Mission compound the day this family were leaving to go back to their town. They had with them their companion schoolteacher. The two women smiled at me in playful giggles as they disappeared under their burkas. Three adults and four children squeezed into a rather small battered car for the journey. The baby was nursed on her mother's knee. They waved and called a laughing good-bye as the car moved out of the compound and through the gateway and turned into the dusty lane. I prayed in earnest for their safety for the roads can be dangerous with insurgents. A foreign aid worker had been killed on an outlying road prior to my arrival in Mazar-e-Sharif.

With the daily routine of Dari lessons and tutoring at the College coming to a close there was great cause for thanks to our Father. The teacher I assisted with tutorials, asked probing questions concerning my faith. The good-bye to my teacher of Dari brought opportunity for his search to be ongoing when I had left. Within the cultural and religious confines God lays His hand on those who will belong to Him. In an email home to praying friends and family I wrote:

'Reading the book of Luke this morning I came to the final words: "And they worshipped Him and returned to Jerusalem with great joy"
Luke 24:52"

I was thankful all over again that the One we trust is ALIVE!. The word 'Mazar' interpreted means 'grave' and 'Mazar-e-Sharif' means 'Grave of the Sharif' a noble leader who is believed to be buried under the magnificent Blue mosque here in the city. How different hearts become when we know that our worshipped One is alive! This is my closing week of my time here, and it has been deeply encouraging in many ways. I am so grateful to you for praying for me. I am just one servant like you are, but how wonderful to know God entrusts us with bold gestures for His sake, wherever we are.

The opportunity to teach young women and to engage in some significant conversation with them opened up this week. The teacher I supported expressed her gratitude for the tutoring of the students. A photo was taken of her and me on the swing in the College courtyard.

A valued woman here in the Women's Centre is Marzia who cooks for the staff. She creates a magnificent vegetable soup dolloped generously with rich Afghan yoghurt topped with pomegranate juice. I had a sweet time with her and the only mature-age student in my class on my last day. We sat in the pleasant atmosphere of the courtyard when again the name of Jesus came into our conversation.

I was given a farewell early Christmas meal last night by three of my foreign aid worker friends. I have been utterly indulged, in this last week. What a blessing after some heavy ploughing! God is so merciful and these last days have opened up possibilities if He wills for a return trip later next year. Alot needs to be committed to prayer for His open doors to be made clear.

Saturday I leave for home arriving late Sunday night. It sounds a novelty to be warm. I hear you are having weather very different from here. The last few days have mercifully not been windy or icy. Just icy nights and early mornings. I have eight layers of warmth including a ski hat worn to bed in order to sleep easily. The cold air bites one's face.

I look forward to sharing with you face to face. Love and thank you for following these journals. I have added one last glimpse of evening light in Afghanistan.

In His love and care and mercy.'

The N.G.O. Director's wife expressed their desire for me to *"please come back and help with the English teaching"*. They were soon to leave Afghanistan after what would be, by then,12 years of serving by them. Such cheerful endurance in this family. When I expressed the desire to go into the Women's Prison on a subsequent trip, they directed me to another Non-Government Organisation to make enquiries of them.

For now it was time to return home to my loved ones.

It was still a dark night when the taxi tooted its horn and Faisal the doorkeeper opened the gate for me on my last early morning in Mazar. The Director gave me a grateful farewell, and insisted on helping me into the taxi. The night before, his wife had come to say goodbye. She was dressed in a magnificent jewelled shalwar chemise. She was off to a wedding. She looked beautiful. I was so grateful for their having sheltered me in their home for this month.

In the early dark I waved to the Director and Faisal the doorkeeper.

The taxi was stopped at five security checkpoints before entering the Mazar airport precincts. A blinding torch at one was shone in my face as I was sitting in the back. With an abrupt command the policeman asked for the boot of the taxi to be opened. I was relieved he didn't want me to open up my suitcase. It was too early in the morning to be intelligent and understand that he was simply doing his job.

Once in the airport acreage I was directed to a portable building in the open land quite some distance from the last final entrance checkpoint. I was to be scanned for dangerous weapons. As a woman it would be done in a separate space. With some shared beams of light from the security checkpoint I walked through uncut grass. My boots made a crunch on the brittle icy ground. I stepped up into the simple cabin. There, sitting by a fire burning in a wood-fired stove, was a woman of early middle years. She was hardly shielded from the weather as the door remained open. The temperature was near to or below zero. She looked cold and sad. It occurred to me she was probably a widow to necessitate working in this bleak setting.

She completed checking me for security purposes. Using my rudimentary Dari and gestures, I learnt she was a widow as I had imagined. Why else would she be working in such extreme conditions during the night? I asked about her children. Putting my palms together in a gesture of prayer I asked her could I pray for her? She nodded a sad smile.

I held her and prayed for her for the Lord to minister into her needs, for her and her family.

I asked Father God for a revelation of His reality and love for her. She wiped tears from her eyes. I thanked her and tucked into her hand a gift from my brothers and sisters back home. Widows work for very little. I often think of her, even still. I know she was on God's heart as He has said so in His Word.

While the security police at the checkpoint did not ask for my suitcase to be opened, this time at the airport it was necessary. Everything was rummaged through. When he discovered some knitting in my carry-on luggage, the officer held it up high and in theatrical horror said *"What is this !?"* He stared in alarm at the points of my circular knitting needle holding my half-completed rug high above his shoulders.

"I am a grandmother" taking the rug from his hands and knitting a few stitches to show him.

"Okay, okay" he respectfully nodded. With a sweet kind of reverence he slowly and carefully folded the rug and needle, placing it neatly with care into my small luggage bag.

With deep concentration he slowly closed the zipper. Grandmothers are held in high esteem. I think I must be one of very few who have been allowed to take a knitting needle onto an aircraft. I was grateful for the grace I was given and said when he handed back my carry-on bag:

"Thank you"

When the call came to board, we walked out quite a distance across a broad tarmac to the waiting aircraft. Ahead of me rose close mountains dusted with snow. Rays of first light tipped the peaks in silver. I stopped in the silence to watch blades of rising gold cut icy shafts through the ravines. In awe all I could utter was: *"Thank You Father"*

33.

DEPARTURE

The plane flew 300 kms south-eastward across a mountainous wilderness cloaked in snow. On arrival in Kabul there were some hours to fill in before my flight to Dubai in the late afternoon. I was to be picked up and taken to a mission guesthouse to spend the day resting.

At arrival Kabul airport, a thoughtful gesture was made by two American engineers from Utah. We had flown on the same flight from Mazar-e-Sharif. They noticed I was sitting in an open waiting space at the airport and were troubled for my safety. One of them came and appealed to me to come with them for protection. We walked quite a distance out of the airport region to a pick-up point where a crowd had been halted and refused entry any closer. Such were the security measures that day. I appreciated their concern. I understood it as the Lord's hand yet again keeping me safe. The airport is regarded as a non-safe area, and this was proven only weeks after I was there. Insurgents blew up a building on the boundary not far from where I was sitting alone. Many were killed.

I was able to spend the day in the mission guesthouse in Kabul. Sitting on the upstairs balcony I had an expansive view of the rooftops veiled that day in a thick smog. Pollution was heavy. Even covering one's nose and mouth helped only slightly. Below me was a backyard of washing hanging on the line, a dog sniffing, another lying in the sun. A child called to its mother. It was a regular day in a city which is now considered over- crowded. Because of the war in outlying provinces, many have migrated to the city leaving it choked with traffic and insubstantial infrastructure.

As planned we left for the airport in good time but chaos easily reigns on their roads. An official visitor arriving at the airport was given priority and so one main outgoing road from the airport was closed for the cavalcade. The remaining road had to be shared by traffic going both ways. It was mayhem. Drivers dived this way and that way to take an opportune space to move. My driver mounted the median strip and zoomed up to squeeze into a minimal space ahead. Arriving at the airport gate we could go no further. Vehicles from three directions were jammed.

I offered to get out and walk but was forbidden.

"*Too dangerous!*" said my driver.

We sat, and sat, and waited, and then sat longer. I was beginning to really believe I would miss my flight. It was then I remembered how valuable it is to sing praises to God in the midst of a dilemma. I then launched into singing every worship song I could think of. It wasn't very convincing enthusiasm that I offered the Father. I knew He knew we were stuck.

I even tried to mathematically work it out if I was undoing the traffic jam. It reminded me of trying to unravel an impossible knot in wool or cotton thread. Nothing helped. We were still going nowhere when an officer appeared by our vehicle which was right in the centre of the knot.

He had impressive gold braid on his shoulders which indicated they had called in a chief traffic official. He knew what to do, and gently and masterfully edged by directions each vehicle this way, then that way. What a marvel to watch him! I was so relieved when we could move and pass through the entrance gates only just in time to board for my flight home. Again, *Thank You Father!*

34.

POSTSCRIPT

There are times when we need to accept disappointment. As much as I desired to return to Afghanistan, not only to teach in the College again, but also to enter the Women's Prison in Mazar-e-Sharif, it wasn't to be. Both organisations managing these projects from their international head-offices made a fresh ruling. In the light of increasing threats to workers' safety, a policy was established of no more short-term workers in danger zones.

I grieved over the closed door, but understood that while I had been protected on numerous occasions, there was no surety that this would continue. God knows the limits of our earthly time, and when one door closes, His next for us opens. A compounding factor was that the Women's College where I had taught, was closed in the following year after many successful years of enabling women to be educated.

Praying for many months for the women in prison in Afghanistan brought some happy news. A young woman I had worked with closely in Mazar, came to faith and responded to the need in the prison for literacy classes for the older women. Being a local woman, now in faith, it was so appropriate that one of the Lord's own Dari-speaking servants could easily gain entrance. It eased my disappointment.

An email from those still in Mazar told me the winter was the coldest for 50 years. Many bodies were found frozen to death in the streets. I wondered about the woman in the dishevelled burka whose hand I had held. Did she survive? Only the Father knows.

I searched for other opportunities to work with Afghan women, in other countries, but no door opened. There are many Afghan and other refugees in many cities around the world.

God has servants who respond with willing hearts. It is His work. It is His kingdom He is establishing. He searches for worshiping hearts and minds to be vigilant to where He needs His children to go. It is only by His empowering sustaining grace that enables us to obey if He calls.

PART 5
2016

35.

WHAT NEXT?

I appreciated keeping in touch with those I had met on my ventures to other cultures. Two very valued friends who I first met in Pakistan were now living in China. Three years had passed since endeavouring to return to Afghanistan. I had settled in my heart the fact I could not return. I had come to accept my age was possibly an indicator of needing to be content to stay at home. God had a surprise for me.

In an email from my friends in China they included a delightful photo of their believing friends with whom they met regularly. Immediately I experienced a quickening in my heart for these young Chinese students studying to prepare for whatever God might have them do in the future. I recounted this to my friends in a return email. Swiftly came their reply:

"*Come!*"

It seemed so unlikely, so out of the question financially. While I am deeply grateful for my Age Pension there was hardly money left over for planning another overseas trip. When I wrote back that I could hardly see it happening soon, but I would love to be there, again they replied:

"*Come!*"

In a strange heavenly moment while endeavouring to understand God's purposes in this invitation, I was tidying up some old books and papers in my home. My father long since with the Lord, had gathered some copies of "China's Millions". They were bound books of Hudson Taylor's China Inland Mission letters and reports from the field in the 19th Century.

My father had photocopied some of the pages for whatever purpose I didn't know. These were among the stray papers I was endeavouring to put away in orderly fashion. I glanced quickly at the page right there in front of me. It was Hudson Taylor's report on their thanksgiving that a base had just been established in a particular area. It was the exact place from which I had now received an invitation. God gives the most unlikely encouragement even while simply tidying up papers! I took it as a '*Yes...this invitation is from the Lord*'. For God His kingdom purposes are not confined to temporal measure. His work He was doing through those young people in China 140 years ago and centuries earlier through others, was continuing. I was yet to see just how wonderfully He is building His kingdom through people responding to Him now. We consider in wonder the growth of God's kingdom in this nation.

I sought support from my family and let friends know what might be possible. I applied for a government Centrelink loan available to pensioners, which covered most of my airfare.

Family and eager supportive friends ladled gifts into my bank account, so generously I was overwhelmed. I booked my airline ticket and in a matter of weeks I was on my way. I was to support the young people in their mastering of English by daily tutorials.

Arriving in China there was great joy in meeting up again with my friends who I hadn't seen since the flood relief season in southern Pakistan six years before. God binds us to each other with an extraordinary love. We drove from the airport in a taxi arriving at an insignificant street in suburban China. There at the entrance to the street was a cluster of students waiting to welcome me.

Down the street, to a door by a restaurant, and up several flights of stairs I was shown to my room. It was where I would stay for the weeks I had committed. The building was an unlikely place to house a vigorous bible college. Thirty young students held their bible lectures and discussions in the second storey. Below on the first storey were housed the more mature graduate students waiting to be sent to different fields of service. These were the ones I would be tutoring.

On the roof was a kitchen and room to eat, open to the cold winter weather. A canvas curtain only partially shielded them from the wind and icy rain. Washing lines under cover at the other end of the roof provided some space for clothes to dry. In between was a vegetable garden.

Because of strict government laws, believers in China have to maintain underground lives.

They refuse to be registered. They desire to stay this way, rather than give priority to the government which demands honouring the rule of government over God's Word. They are a hidden people for Jesus' sake. In every other way they endeavour to be law-abiding peaceful citizens.

Most of the students were from the rural regions predominantly from Henan province from which the underground church first developed. During the cultural revolution they literally were in an underground facility. Much has been written of the emergence of the Church at this time. Now I was with the third generation from these pioneer believers. To listen to their stories of grandparents' and parents', uncles' and aunts' suffering was the deepest education I could imagine. The legacy of faith under persecution has been engraved on their young hearts.

One young woman among my students recalled her elderly aunty who had been imprisoned and tortured for her faith. Another student, a young father, with tears, said he remembered that when he was 4 years old, his grandfather came out of prison. He tried to talk to him, as a young child, but his grandfather never answered him. He was completely mute. He had been so tortured for his faith, he could no longer speak. One of the tutorial students said to me with sober conviction:

"We are carried on the shoulders of the martyrs."

The graduate students I was to tutor were in their early to late twenties. It was their intention to focus on studying the Word, and waiting on God to know where next He would want them to go. Some are preparing for opportunities in areas for which Christians suffer for their faith. God was taking them very patiently and gently through preparatory years. A married couple were expecting their first baby and another couple already had a tiny tot. I was deeply impressed with their zeal to follow Jesus whatever that required of them.

Their worship and prayer times could be heard resonating through the simple hotel facility in which we were housed.

During prayer times they prayed in such earnest and unison that their 'Amen' after each petition travelled like a triumphant shudder through the walls. Their singing was glorious and such an exhortation to praise God.

The building had two atriums to the open sky and corridors had wind whistling through them. The temperature was around minus 6 degrees Celsius so we all were rugged up for open air even inside.

The thirty or so younger college students above on the second floor rose up at 5.00 am each morning for study of the Word and prayer. Breakfast for them was 7.00 am and 8.00am for Bible lectures to begin. In break times they provided raucous joy. They even tried kicking a soccer ball. At evening times the building shook with their rumbles. They lived reclusively, only going out on certain days to minister to the elderly in care homes, or to go to buy food at the markets, then, only in small groups. It was admirable discipline that they managed in this hidden space. How precious to our Father must be this cluster of His children, and others elsewhere in this land, so confined for His sake.

The students encompassed me with generosity. They would not allow me to pay for my room, my food, travel expenses, eating out, nor any extra warm clothes I needed. I was completely provided for in every way. They bought me a small electric heater for my room. No one else in the college had such a thing. It did help in the bleak night temperature, and to bring into the tutorial room for English time.

Each morning on the stroke of 7.00am, there was a knock on my door and one of my students handed me two boiled eggs for my breakfast. He committed to do this each morning setting his alarm to wake up in time to serve me. At lunch he prepared my meal and brought it to me to eat in the warmth of my English teaching room, as I hugged the heater. Likewise he served me an evening meal, so I did not need to eat in the roof kitchen dining area open to the icy weather. I was deeply touched by his servant heart.

There were among my students two young women eager to become competent in English.

They were planning to leave for Ethiopia to study in the Evangelical Bible College. All the lectures were to be in English. They put intense effort into their homework. I decided to give each of them one-to-one tutoring to maximise the limited time before they set off for Addis Ababa. The small group tuition for others worked well for interactive speaking. Of great use were my English lessons I had designed when in Sydney, teaching Afghan women. I did not know all those years before when designing them that I would be using them with young Mandarin-speaking students in China, studying in secret.

On Saturday nights English Corner was held. This is a format right throughout China, where those wanting to improve on their English are encouraged to engage in discussion.

A number of Charities or Non-Government Organisations have found them useful for serving the community. Because the bible college was near a university campus a cluster of university students came for this regular time. It was an effective way of inviting those who did not know the Lord, to experience the company of His children living in community.

We had some lively discussions by which I learnt what the visiting university students were studying, what their hopes and plans were for the future. Even though some of them were adamant in their not believing in God they insisted on coming each Saturday night to improve their English. Lively friendships were formed.

I listened to these young university students who had been offered not even an ethical framework by which to live. I was challenged by what they expressed but encouraged the bible students to explain their faith. It was a vigorous exchange. On the particular evening of discussing Ethics one of the believing college students in response told his testimony.

He spoke in Mandarin for clarity and fluency. His wife gave the translation into English. He described the Word of God being his directive for life.

His was a powerful conversion after a deliberate defiance of his mother's faith for so many years. He then played on his guitar a worship song. There was an attentive silence that night and a noticeable softening in those who contested faith in Christ.

On a particular morning I needed to go out to the shops nearby for some essentials and made sure the door to the street was left unlocked. I was to be out for only a few minutes.

On my return I confidently went to open the door, but it had been locked as someone had gone out shortly after me. I knocked and knocked, but those in the upper floors could not hear me. I tried again, knocking even louder and calling up to the windows above, but to no avail. I was freezing. By then it was well below zero. I had no credit on my phone, so asked a lady could she kindly lend me her mobile to endeavour to ring them, but no one answered the call. I was getting colder. She suggested that three young men walking in the street might be able to help. In Mandarin she asked them for me, would they like to try knocking loudly for someone upstairs to hear. Three young hearty men lent their weight and voices to thumping the door and shouting until someone came down and opened up. It was a relief, so I invited them up for a cup of tea, which they welcomed. I introduced them to some of my students who served them refreshments.

I explained we were a community who love Jesus. They listened politely, and nodded when I invited them to our next English Corner that evening. They were three university students living in accommodation two doors down so it was a small distance to come in response.

That evening just one of the young men came. He listened and took part in our discussion.

He was eager to come again, so was invited by the students to come to their early morning Sunday fellowship the next day. He turned up with enthusiasm. He turned up for the next Saturday night, and the next Sunday morning. One of the young men among the bible graduates obtained a bible for him.

Over weeks he came to regular bible study and learned of the gospel through group study and having it explained to him through friendship. He was in his final year of Accountancy, after which he would be moving back to his family in a distant town. In the remaining months of study at university, I learnt from emails to me after leaving China, that he had become a firm believer in Christ. It was a locked door on a freezing morning that God had used to lay His hand on this young man for His purposes. On our last meeting before I left, we hugged and he said with misty eyes:

"*I will miss you*" He held his Mandarin/English bible close to his chest. We recalled our unlikely meeting in the street.

Christmas Day arrived with the promise of a trip to the city. It was sharply cold as I travelled in a taxi through fog and pollution. My mask would be needed. I was to spend the day with my friends who had invited me to China. As the taxi entered the city it began to snow. A gift of a gentle white drift of flakes fell as I got out of the taxi. I was welcomed into a snug lounge room in a city apartment. Others had gathered also from several different nations. All lovers of Jesus We opened our day together with a Bible Study, and discussion followed by a time of prayer and thanksgiving for Jesus, coming as a babe. God became Man, out of love for the world. The other guests had come as post-graduates from major universities in Uganda, Kenya, Ethiopia, and Korea. Delicious food was laid out. The young man from Korea had shopped and prepared the tastiest dishes simmering over burners on the table.

The day was one of lively chatter.

With reluctance, as dusk was settling, plans were made to get me a taxi for my return to the college. As we waited in the biting chill, I was introduced to an elderly shoe-repair man plying his trade on the city pavement. He stretched out his hand with a smile. By interpretation I was told he had loved Jesus since he was eight years old. It showed in the joyful creases of his face.

In the days that followed there was an invitation to me from the College principal to speak to the thirty or so younger students on the second floor of the college. With a prepared talk, interpreted by one of my competent graduate students, I told them of my upbringing in a Christian home. I told them I had turned away from all I had learnt from the Bible. I rebelled against God. This led to great sorrow in my life. In His mercy God showed me that Jesus His son had died for that very same rebellion and sorrow. He took all that I deserved of God's anger, when He died for me. I urged them to hold onto all that they were learning from the Bible.

"God wants to talk with you personally through His Word, for you to discover for yourself His love and purpose for your life".

I implored them to explore the truth in His Word, and really get to know Jesus for themselves, not just because it was a family tradition. To hold onto Jesus no matter what happens.

"Don't ever give up, no matter how hard it is".

They listened intently. I prayed for them:

"That Lord Jesus You would keep them in Your Name".

Days folded into one another, and the graduate students I was tutoring made great progress in their English. I was so heartened to know this limited time was proving a benefit to them. My joy over being with them and participating in their fellowship times was unexpectedly interrupted.

In the complete dark, during the night as I was getting out of bed, I managed to hit my head against the strangely shaped bedhead where I was sleeping. I hit it with such force I managed to displace two discs in my neck and dislocate my shoulder. On reflection I believe I was slightly concussed as well, as it was some time before I could recall how it had happened. The pain was agonizing but help was given. By a bus-ride into the University Hospital in the city, and careful negotiation by one of my students, I was given a voucher to be seen by the appropriate doctors.

In a multi-storeyed facility with a multitude of consultation rooms on many floors, the scene was comparable with a humming international airport. Ever-moving escalators carried crowds to the various levels. Only God could have organised that as well as being given a magnetic resonance examination, and prescriptive medication, I had the blessing of a consultation with a doctor who loved Jesus. He completed his consultation by praying for me. He also prescribed medication as well as recommending a collar to support my neck. I was grateful.

My students watched over me with concerned care. I soon was comforted despite the pain. I persevered for some days but the medication made me so drowsy as to indicate it would be better to go home. I could hardly teach the tutorials while so drowsy on medication. It meant two weeks earlier than I had planned. It did have a hidden blessing for the students as it was soon to be Chinese New Year. It meant the students could return to their families for this all-important celebration. Two of the students were engaged to be married, and it meant they would have an extra two weeks with their respective families before marriage.

I reluctantly packed my bags and we planned for the trip to the airport for the following morning. The evening before leaving I shared a meal with the students in the kitchen- dining area up on the roof. We all rugged up against the below zero temperature and huddled around a fire. They crouched on the floor in their traditional style. Sad farewells were made after five weeks of deep and informative companionship.

I had gained an understanding of my Chinese brothers' and sisters' lives as believers in an ever-threatening political environment. I had observed their steadfast grip on Jesus, and His undeniable presence in them and with them. I became convinced that while we enjoy a freedom in Australia, to worship and follow Christ, we can be utterly unaware of what faith requires of brothers and sisters in a hostile political setting. Even as I write I understand that believers in Henan province have recently had their church raided with many members being taken away to Re-Education Camps. China has entered a new phase for those who follow Jesus. It is cause for great concern and urgent prayer for our brothers and sisters contending with opposition.

36.

SOMETHING ELSE 2017

If I thought my overseas mission trips had come to completion, I was mistaken. The same friends who invited me to China, told me of a school which was being newly established in Gesuba, a township in southern Ethiopia. It was where my Ethiopian brother had been raised as one of the Wolayta people. Along with a group of fellow-believers, a former community facility had been transformed into a school for local children. They were needing help in English teaching. It was to be of Infant's level classes, with a hope of expanding to higher grades as it developed.

In Ethiopia, all teaching at High School level is done in English, hence the early start in Infant's School. The small school opened in the Autumn and I was asked would I be able to go and help, even for a few weeks. With the confidence that I had seen God move in my last unlikely venture to China, I made plans and within a few weeks, flew out to Addis Ababa, the capital of Ethiopia. I committed to a month's stay.

I was met at the airport by members of the fellowship from the underground church in China. Here in the capital of Ethiopia, Addis Ababa a cluster of them live in a community house in a suburb of this bustling, dusty city. All are there by the call of God for kingdom purposes, seven in all, including two of my students who I had tutored in China. Three others in the household were studying at the Ethiopian Missionary Bible College in Durame further south. They were spending some weeks break in Addis, in the community house. The rest were studying at the Evangelical Theological College.

What a joyous re-union it was with the two young women who were my former students in China. The married couple leading this team welcomed me into their shared home. Their two children provided the chatter and activity that only children bring. They had also taken in two unwanted puppies, who had been discovered abandoned. With children and two tiny dogs running around our feet, along with seven adults, the house invited connection. Someone was always, coming or going.

Isaac, my Chinese brother in Christ heading the household, suggested that I spend one week with them in the capital, after which the three Durame College students along with me, would travel south to the school in Gesuba. I needed to trust the remaining three weeks would be sufficient time to provide adequate support to the teachers, in teaching English. These few initial days helped me familiarise myself with my Chinese companions.

The team going to Gesuba, would comprise the two young men, Caleb and David, whose wives were back in China caring for their children. They were waiting for when each of them could welcome their wife and children to Ethiopia. I marvelled at their patience despite missing their loved ones. The third member of our team would be a young Chinese woman, Almaz, who had mastered conversational Amheric, the official Ethiopian language. She came to be a valuable person being able to interpret local's comments and intentions. What I didn't know was, that she had taken one of the squealing puppies as her own. We would be taking him\her on our Gesuba adventure.

Before setting off to the south, with a few days in the capital, I expressed the desire with Isaac, our leader, that I would love to visit the Fistula Hospital in Addis Ababa. Since its inception my family had been closely involved.

Wonderfully, Isaac offered to take me to the Hospital in the city to see if I could visit Dr. Catherine, now alone without her husband. Dr. Reg Hamilin had passed away many years before. Back in the 70's my brother-in-law with the help of others, raised the monies to get the first ward built for the Fistula Hospital. As a younger one, I went with Robert to a meeting in Sydney where Reg Hamlin showed a slide from a projector, of the block of land he and Catherine had purchased in Addis Ababa. It was their vision to establish a hospital exclusively devoted to the young women, who suffered from the terrible injuries from obstructed labour. The establishment of the hospital is a story of one couple's utter devotion to bring relief to women injured and socially ostracised. I was grateful when Isaac suggested he take me into the city and find the Fistula Hospital, with a view to visiting Dr. Catherine.

It was a joy-filled prospect as we wove our way through jumbled city traffic and drove under a huge concrete freeway. We found the street which led down the hill to a quiet tree-lined laneway to the

Hospital. The grounds were landscaped with a sloping lawn bordered by an array of shrubs and flowers. Nooks of seasonal bloom sheltered under wide arching trees. It was as a garden of Eden.

The reception desk made a phone call to Dr. Catherine, relaying my desire to visit her.

Graciously came her happy response. A rose-garden lined the path in a steep descent to her cottage. She was standing in her doorway ready to greet us. Isaac and I received the warmest welcome. We were invited to come in and sit down in her sitting room.

Enjoying a cup of tea together, I explained, while in my younger years, I went with my brother-in-law to a meeting of no more than five people to hear her husband speak. He told us of their vision they had to build a hospital for fistula sufferers. Her face lit up in youthful recall. I told her I can still remember the photo of vacant land, sloping with just one tree on it. She laughed and said:

"You are right! There was only one tree, and it fell down! Now look at the grounds, full of trees so large and beautiful."

She continued to narrate what those early days were like. Wistfully she recalled:

"Addis Ababa was a shanty town then, now look at it!"

Dr. Catherine, though almost 94 when I visited her that day, still made two daily ward rounds. While she can no longer operate, she still takes an attentive interest in all that happens in the hospital. She described their delight in establishing a home further down the slope for girls to return to when they again become pregnant, after a repaired fistula.

They are instructed to come early in their subsequent pregnancy, and stay as residents for the term of their confinement. This is to ensure that their bodies can sustain a whole healthy pregnancy and delivery. Her face melted in compassion when she spoke about the mothers. I saw a group of them sitting in the gentle Autumn sun on the surrounds to the hospital. They were weaving baskets and chatting to each other.

I explained to her my plans for the month, teaching in a tiny school newly established in Gesuba in the south. She listened with great interest. She engaged eagerly with Isaac, as one who had come from the underground church in China. She quizzed him on his life in China. It was an intimate time with Dr. Catherine, talking about family, and grandchildren, and how she would love me to come again when my teaching was completed. Isaac enabled me again to visit her before I returned to Australia. I was deeply grateful for her warmth. She is delightfully down-to-earth and humble. She has a wry and wonderful sense of humour. She stood at the door and waved us off until we were out of sight.

The day came for us to make the journey to Gesuba. Firstly, the plans were to drive to Durame where my three team companions were to collect more belongings including the essential cooking gear. There we were to be transferred to a hired minibus for the mountainous trip to Gesuba. We were to stay in a guesthouse. It sounded quite convenient.

To quote from my first email home to those praying for us, from Gesuba I wrote:

> *"From high up in the beautiful mountains of Gesuba, Ethiopia, I write at midnight woken by a zealous chant from someone close-by.*

Perhaps it is a Muslim prayer as it is the first few minutes of a Holy Day today for them. Earlier in the evening someone next door kept waking me with enthusiastic Hallelujahs, so there you have the diversity of faith in this town.

On arrival in Addis Monday last week my luggage stayed in Singapore, collected the next day. Contrary to expectations I spent all last week in Addis with my Chinese team-mates.

We left in the early dark hours Sunday for the city of Sodo then to Durame in the South to see the sunrise over the deep purple mountains and sweeping savannah plains! It was breathtakingly beautiful with gilded clouds.

On arrival in Durame we swapped vehicles for a minibus for the rough mountain journey to Gesuba. All up 11 hours on the road and totally worth it!

Ethiopia's natural mountain beauty is stunning in its sunrise and sunset.

There is a hush to the beginning and close of each day.

The guesthouse where we planned to stay had been given to others. Swift change of plans means we are now living in the school compound. We are learning to be in view for considerable hours and schoolyard squeals a constant background.

Gesuba is a lost town as recounted by a brother in Christ who is a native of the town. As we have walked some of the streets with a cluster of children, my Chinese companion and I had opportunity to pray for its people, so loved by God at extraordinary cost in Jesus. As we asked the children "Do you know Jesus?" translated by Caleb my Chinese brother, we got a wonderful response from one little girl. When asked, she sang a Jesus song. Others joined in and adults came to check out what was happening. Caleb who speaks Amheric quizzed the little girl who confidently explained Jesus' death for our sin, His resurrection and rising to glory! A real preacher, about 12 years old. Spot on!

That was our first spontaneous mission into Gesuba! What fun! We hope to do this when we have spare moments.

Teaching began on Monday with a bang! The children are from poor homes and squealed and shrieked with delight when I brought out the textas and coloured pencils. The teaching rooms are small and children are squashed into 3 to a desk. It is all so intense and wild and wonderful.

Every now and then I have to step outside to get a fresh breath of air and pray "please Lord help me".

Most of all I pray that they will understand God's making them and His love for them and all He has created. I am teaching "All Things Bright and Beautiful" just as I did in Pakistan, giving rich vocabulary and inspiring the greatest artwork. I love what they draw and bring to me with such eagerness.

I pray you are encouraged in your prayers for us here, my Chinese brothers and sister with me. Ephraim, an Ethiopian brother from Durame has joined us. Ephraim will keep me company next week when the Chinese team have to return to Durame Bible College for exams. I am so deeply encouraged in Christ by my brothers and sister in this team. I am deeply touched by their constant care and consideration...."

The days teaching were exacting every ounce of strength I could muster. I had prepared before coming to Gesuba, two felt banners to be hung in their classroom. In K-Mart purchased plywood alphabet letters, I had sewn on each banner the first two lines of the ancient hymn. After each lesson the 1st and 2nd class children's handmade artwork reflecting the lesson was attached to the felt.

Almaz stayed up with me at nights sewing or glueing each zealously created object to the banners. Just as we would be really getting 'into it' the electricity would go out, and we would continue in limited streams of light from my torch and Almaz's solar-powered lamp.

To make it slightly calamitous Almaz's puppy she had brought from Addis, skipped and wriggled around our feet in the half-light. We just hoped he hadn't poo-ed somewhere under our feet, in the dark.

The principal appointed to oversee the school would only call in for a short while each day.

This was a secondary appointment as he was a high-school teacher in the town. He cautioned me that I must not teach Bible. Government policy was, that unless it was registered as a Christian school, this was not allowed. I responded by explaining the words of the hymn I was teaching them. I also told him I had taught this in another culture to children of other faiths, and no protest was made from parents or authorities. He was satisfied, so the nights sewing and gluing continued.

Single word vocabulary was enlarged into phrases in English. A book was purchased for each child to write the day's lesson. They loved writing. They were hungry for writing. I loved watching their intensity as they managed in varying degrees of competency to master the task then bring me their work with such pride. Shy pride in some. I asked them to come to me one-by-one and read to me out of their writing books. This gave me a quiet opportunity to pray for them individually.

I saw some answers to those prayers in the weeks I was teaching. Timid ones grew in confidence and frightened ones came to peace. One child was very quiet, but intelligent by the work he gave me. Tears were in his eyes, when I prayed for him, and I wondered whether he was treated harshly at home, or whether he had experienced some deep loss.

His clothes were very poor. Father God wanted him to know he was loved, that He delighted in who He had made him to be. I told him so. I told him he was a clever boy and never be afraid to be a clever boy, to keep learning and to grow in knowledge. I sensed God's hand on his life, that He would fulfil all that He intended for him.

In moments while teaching the 2nd class, and the lesson was going well, a child would suddenly decide to climb out the window. The class teacher swiftly followed with a branch of soft willow-tree in her hand, in determined pursuit. While heads were down and elbows shuffled for room in the limited desk space, we could hear the squeals of delight from the truant being chased around the playground. He was enjoying the game, until it ended in verbal discipline.

As the days progressed, each line and verse of "All Things Bright & Beautiful" was eagerly expanded in their writing books. I taught them to sing the lesson being taught, with gestures. They loved singing. They loved yelling too, so moderation was encouraged so they could think about what they were singing. As I travelled through the villages on a trip one Saturday to the city of Sodo, I saw village children running half-naked, climbing, shouting and chasing goats and calves around their clearance. I realised the children I was teaching were utterly free-range in every way. How well my cluster of students were doing when they kept sitting and listening, writing and drawing, all in a limited space. No wonder some of them wanted to yell "All Things & Beautiful" or got the impulse to climb out the window.

The 1st class teacher was a lover of Jesus and her teaching and her students reflected a grace and respect which made the task of teaching her class so much easier. They had an extra door they could escape through mid-lesson, but as far as I can recall none took the opportunity. She appreciated my opening the lesson with a prayer for Jesus to help us as I did each day for 2nd class. They had their own felt banner which they cherished, and celebrated by pointing out their particular creation which was now sewn or glued. They loved adding to it. Progressively they took increasing delight to see it slowly covered with all the things that God had made.

Each lunch hour with a few exceptions, the children would walk home, then return for the afternoon. Even though it was winter at almost 6,000 feet altitude, the closeness to the Equator brought some hot days. Some children lived closer to the school but others walked as far as a mile home and a mile back to school. Except for really hot days when they stayed at home for the afternoon, most pupils walked there and back twice a day.

Little ones who stayed for lunch came to school carrying their distinct Ethiopian containers of lunch. What looked like a miniature billy-can with a lid, swung in their hand, while a very second-hand schoolbag hung from their shoulders.

For many the opportunity to be going to school was held as a great honour. In every other way, they were simply children, playful, competitive, energetic, sometimes eager to learn, sometimes restless and naughty but so loveable. When I needed to lie down midday, they revelled in banging on my door and calling "Teacher, teacher" which needed some patience and grace. I knew this was a limited time, and I needed to keep loving them, no matter how exhausted I felt some days. After my interrupted "lie down" I had another class and another hour of teaching, so I needed grace for them. Each time they saw me crossing the school playground to come to their room, the 2nd class children would burst into singing "All Things Bright & Beautiful" just in case I had forgotten.

My Chinese companions had come simply to watch over me, interpret where needed and shop and cook their unique meals. While I taught the children, they filled their hours with sharpening their English with Ephraim tutoring them. Ephraim, an Ethiopian University student, spoke perfect Cambridge English. He was a valuable companion to interpret in my conversations with the school staff.

In the weeks they were with us the Chinese team took turns to do the cooking. Rural Chinese cuisine is nutritious and tasty.

Midday was our main mealtime, and the call "*Marion, lunch!*" were the most welcome words to hear. Our times chatting around the dinner table and our early morning bible and prayer times before the tasks of the day were not to be missed. Subtle differences in humour added colour to our times together.

There was great cause for laughter when we finally 'got' each other. Chinese seem to have a gift for minimal words to maximum effect.

Our valued meal times together had to be interrupted by our Chinese companions having to return to Durame Missionary College for their exams.

For the week it was just Ephraim and I in the school, we needed to do our own shopping and cooking. I learnt how not to be too troubled by purchasing meat hanging in the open, with a large carpet of flies tasting it first. I asked Ephraim:

"*Is that normally the way?*" He answered with a polite nod. I took extra care cutting up the lamb that night, exorcising every bit of fat and surface the flies had fancied. We didn't get sick, so all was well.

Shopping in the market for fruit and vegetables was a treat. The potatoes when cooked tasted like those I had as a child when my father and mother were vegetable farmers in the Southern Highlands of New South Wales. They were so earthy and nutty, without sprays nor genetically modified, but simply cultivated by hard-working hands in the rich red soil of Gesuba. Those and the crisp mountain-grown cabbages were a delight to cut and minimally cook and eat, or simply eat raw. Tomatoes were the same.

Ephraim and I enjoyed our meals together, along with my education in meat-shopping.

He smiled at my naïve alarm. He didn't demur when I vomited into the earthen corner of the out-door coffee shop. I had inadvertently drunk river water with my regular medication and added powerful anti-biotics to the fine Ethiopian coffee. I had managed to have a tick embedded in my leg, hence the anti-biotics. It did come out, so all was well.

Ephraim and I really enjoyed reading the Word together and praying before the start of each day.

When it was time for our Chinese companions to return to the school, he and I made plans to travel into Sodo city to meet up with them halfway. We were to meet in a super-style tourist hotel.

It required us boarding quite a small, well-worn bus to take us down the mountain from Gesuba and then up a mountain to Sodo city. Every inch of the way was accompanied by loud amplified Ethiopian rock music. Heavy luggage on the roof of the small bus meant we tilted at a precarious angle at enthusiastic speed. The road was not built for two vehicles passing. One had to yield to the other. Our bus chose the verge of the road and the dust, swaying in alarming rhythm to the pulse of the rock beat. I had the benefit of a seat next to the driver, while Ephraim got the worst of the swaying and hurtling in the back of the bus. He got out looking rather unwell. The journey down the mountain and then up to Sodo was a series of passing through intermittent dust clouds all to music.

It made the hotel in Sodo look extra super, and the Ethiopian coffee while sitting under a large tree, like a dream. The aroma of Balsa wood burning in the large bowl by our table added an exquisite peace to meeting up with our Chinese companions. They were relieved for having completed their Durame Missionary College exams.

On our return to Gesuba we were invited to visit the parents of the Ethiopian brother in Christ, who had helped in establishing the school. His parents lived out of town. With eagerness I waited for our transport of what I anticipated was a small van to accommodate the five of us. I came out of the school gate to see five motor bikes and their riders waiting.

I was invited to sit on the back of the remaining waiting rider and his bike. I paused in alarm at the thought of riding pillion to the farm down the mountainside. I had ridden pillion in Quetta, Pakistan but that was on level roads. Even then I was scared as the driver swooped and dived in and out of fast- moving traffic.

In convoy the five of us travelled through the town and down a steep and winding road.

We had no leathers, no helmet and the confident bike rider who took me, had to cope with me yelling "Jesus!" as we sped down a long, long hill and leaning to go around a deep bend creating a dust and gravel storm. I was terrified. I was thinking *"This is the day I am going to die!"* I was sliding all over the slippery vinyl seat so held onto his belt loops, determined that if I came off he was coming with me. To enter the gates of the farm and come to a gentle halt beside their farmhouse was a foretaste of heaven.

My Ethiopian friend's elderly parents were standing in the front garden to welcome us and draw us into their generous loungeroom. An array of food waited for us! A table was spread with several spiced hot dishes with cold accompaniments to add. Ethiopian bread was arranged in rolls on a platter. It is the traditional way of eating to use the bread to scoop up the food. We ate to our utter satisfaction as our hostess begged us to eat more.

Ethiopian hospitality is gentle and persuasive. The aroma of home-grown, home- roasted and ground coffee being brewed over embers, filled the room.

Replete, it was time for a stroll out to their plantation on the hillside. Lush green banana groves decked our path down towards the river. Beyond were the coffee groves. We could hear the river trickling at the bottom of the hill. These Gesuba hills seemed as a slice of Eden. My Ethiopian friend's father is an award-winning farmer acknowledged by the Ethiopian government for his successful organic farm, cleverly terraced on the sloping mountainside. We were the most privileged guests that day.

It was difficult to say good-bye but a semi-trailer was waiting to take us home. I preferred the ride home, comfortably seated, all five of us with the driver in his massive cabin. I was spared a repeat of the terror of a speedy motor bike ride. I didn't slide anywhere nor need to yell to *"Jesus!"* to get safely back home to the school.

As the days drew closer to complete my time in the school, it was my intention to purchase some resources for the school that I could leave with them. The generous gifts given me from home, by friends and family made this possible. In the late afternoon I walked to the township to make the purchase of a good supply of exercise books, pencils, rubbers, rulers and pencil sharpeners. After making the transaction and turning to walk home, a group of teenagers in a pack overwhelmed me. One had his hands in my backpack and another was trying to get into my pocket. I pushed them away, rebuking them sternly and went on my way. The dusk in Gesuba brings a peace, a reflective pause. The teenagers rushing at me had broken into that so harshly. I was almost home, and looking forward to our evening meal when I put my hand in my large pocket for my mobile phone. It was no longer there.

Ephraim insisted we must go to the Police and report it. Instead of sitting around a meal table that evening we walked in semi-darkness to the police-station. I felt sadness more for the kids who habitually steal out of poverty. A phone cashed in at the local mobile phone shop yields quite a sum for them. It is a regular occurrence I was told.

It was to have been a special meal shared that evening with a young Jamaican-American woman working in Gesuba with the American Peace Corps. She was an English teacher employed in the local primary and high school. Natasia was to be taking over the English teaching when I left.

We prayed for the young men as we finally sat down for our late-night dinner when there was a knock on the iron gate of the School. My Ethiopian friend who had established the school, was well known in the town. His brother had received a phone-call. The caller said that he had the phone belonging to the *'forengi'* (foreigner) at the school. Some person, perhaps the mobile shop-owner, must have viewed my photos to identify me. We didn't know quite how it happened. The caller also said he had the thief!

In the dark evening, my Ethiopian friend's brother came through the gate, stretching his hand out to me with the phone. It was an unexpected relief. I asked could I speak to the boy, but he didn't want to face me. He hid behind the iron fence out of sight by the gate. I asked could my message be passed onto him, that I forgave him. I wanted him to know that Jesus loves him. A strange fear fell on the town. Everyone knows when something happens there. No one had ever heard of a thief returning stolen goods.

The Administrator of the province got word of the robbery and rang the next day to apologise to the *'forengi lady'* (foreign lady) for such a shameful thing happening to someone who had come to help their children. I was touched by that word. The police also rang to say how sorry they were. There was a quiet, profound sense of the presence of God over the township. Everyone knew it had happened. The town is so small and a collective conscience had been touched *Thank You Father!*

The thief became a focus for continuing prayer among us, him, and others like him, the 'lost' of Gesuba. "*Please Jesus, may Your kingdom come to this town, and in particular, the young*" were the substance of our prayers.

Before my English teaching came to an end, I wanted to give the children the fun of creating their own small gardens. I figured the best way was to purchase eight bright orange plastic garbage tins and with the help of the school guard filled them with soil.

I had brought from home a number of packets of nasturtium and zinnia seeds. On the day trip to Sodo I had purchased some plants of hibiscus, geranium, and roses for the children to plant along with the seeds. It enhanced our English lessons together, as they took turns to sprinkle seeds, to plant and to water and learn the words. They revelled in this activity and guarded their gardens in great earnest.

Each writing book was filled with the stages of planting, watering and the anticipation of watching the seeds emerge and grow. Hopefully the plants grew and budded to give the children joy. I didn't want them disappointed. I asked Father God for His mercy in this, for the day was fast approaching to say goodbye.

For my last day with the children, Caleb, David, Almaz and Ephraim came into the classrooms to say goodbye. The children had shared their playground with us so generously. They had watched us clean our teeth, wash our dishes, our faces, our clothes. Our shirts and socks and teatowels flapped on the washing lines across from their classrooms. They had played and squeeled with Almaz's puppy on a rope. They didn't know that when they went home each day, we sat on their swings and had a go on their roundabout.

For the team to come into the children's classroom brought a response of awe. Caleb, without knowing the rule about not sharing Bible with the students, gave a lesson about God's Son Jesus. He explained the gospel story in a way the children could comprehend. He spoke in English, with Ephraim translating each phrase into their language of Amheric. The children were transfixed. You could hear a pin drop.

"Thank You Father for that sweet interval"

The staff gave us a ceremonial afternoon coffee farewell. Balsa perfume wafted up from the bowls laid near our feet on the ground, and curtains were hung from the trees to create a 'room'. Mats made from soft grassy reeds were placed on the ground to cover the dirt. The graciousness with which we were served was a ministry of Jesus all of its own.

The teacher who loved Jesus gave a tearful speech. She was particularly sad we were going. I was sad too. I wished Ethiopia wasn't so far away and I could visit them again.

How richly I was blessed by their humility and ability to be taught and directed by me. I had been given so much freedom to share what I could with them.

It was now time to board a bus for another hurtling rock concert down the mountain, back to Sodo and a connecting bus to Durame. There Isaac met us in his comfortable car for the journey back to Addis, but not before sitting down to two meals in that town. One was with the elderly parents of my Ethiopian sister in China. Her parents had been missionaries. Quiet, deep, faithful hearts welcomed us. Her father, then her mother prayed for us. It was a privilege to be in their home and sit with them in the stillness of Christ's presence. Their endurance in faith had wrought a softness of grace and humility.

Our final meal in Durame before leaving was in Ephraim's parent's home. His mother, a gentle woman was carefully sensitive to our needs. Her food, and his father's interest in all we had been doing in the school was encouraging. It was time to say goodbye to Ephraim. He knew I deeply valued him, for his essential support for me while teaching. I couldn't have managed without his translating.

By arrival in Addis we were relieved. The journey had been arduous for Isaac. The roads were rough and semi-trailers forced us off the road into deep culverts. He did remarkably well and was patient, but exhausted, as the car was driven into the driveway of their community house. My Chinese brothers and sisters were such a ministry to me of Father God's care and faithfulness. On the days left before I flew out, my two students from China, now studying theology in Addis, took me on a tour of the Evangelical Theology College in the city.

They showed me the room where they study Academic English, and Theology in another.

They had come so courageously to Ethiopia while young. I was very proud of them, and the work they had invested to get this far in following God's calling. They were two timid students when I taught them in China. I respected their determination to follow Jesus, no matter how challenging in a foreign culture. They were doing well in managing lectures in English. To see their progress was rewarding. To see their joy was even better.

37.

REFLECTION

In sharing these stories with you I want you to know that my chief intention is to describe what God did. In places and events there was an unbroken thread running through each unlikely opportunity. Jesus wanted me to let it be known that He is Alive.

He cares for the widow and the fatherless. He has compassion on those who are in the valley of grief. His heart grieves for a little boy one day running around and then stricken with a crippling disease. His rage is aroused when so many created in His image have been trapped in addiction and then gaoled for theft or illegal practices simply to survive, while their dealer lives extravagantly from the profits. What grief must tear the Father's heart to see a widow bereft of her husband and children, and cast out into the street to beg. He hears the solitary mother with young children, crying out to Him as floodwaters rise around her home.

His heart breaks for those who have not heard of His salvation in Christ, and have no comfort when a loved one is gunned down by insurgents, for the mother whose husband doesn't come home from the fruit market, or a bus-ride to seek work, for the hard-working farmer who has lost his crops in a deluge. Our Father God's heart grieves for the family who has had to flee their home, their livelihood, the familiar, and seek refuge from terror, only to be scorned in the land in which they settle.

He wants them to know His provision for them for eternal safety, in the gift of His Son Jesus who laid down His life for them on a cruel cross. In triumph He rose from death and shares that resurrection joy with those who believe and receive His life.

He broods over His children with protective jealousy when they are threatened or suffer for His sake.

What delight must come for our Father when a small child in a bustling rural city or in a distant mountain village, listens intently when told that he or she is cherished by Him, as the one who made them and that they can become His true child. What joy in heaven when the scriptures are read for the first time, and come to life in one who has had a hunger for truth. Amid a desert of truth, the reality of God and His Son brings a resounding wonder, a light to the eyes like no other.

How little did I imagine when I was utterly broken, and despairing of life in my younger years and navigating the results of my poor judgement and choices, that God would one day in His extraordinary mercy entrust me with these trips. He is so patient with us. I marvel I have been given the privilege of staying where no other Westerner has stayed. I have been welcomed and kept safe where danger prevailed. I have been embraced in shelter by those of a different faith tradition. He has determined this for no other reason than for Jesus to be made known.

Never could I have imagined that I would live with those who worship and study in hiding in order to follow Christ, above all other authorities. To follow in the tracks of their obedience has been an education. To witness what commitment requires of others who have left their home and loved ones long-term for Jesus, is deeply humbling. Some are trusting in Christ where daily danger threatens. They are trusting for safety, not only for themselves, but also for their children, some quite small. It inspires my own desire to be steadfast in faith.

What power is in His gospel. What grace, for anyone who longs for His salvation. He chooses the weak and the foolish to show His glory. I have moments of doubt and at times halting depression. Disappointments have dogged me. I experience sharp aloneness when facing spiritual opposition or the unknown without loved ones. God still entrusts me to keep going. He is faithful and it is He who determines our days. In mercy He set His love upon me. Even as a rebel He pursued me. My prideful heart was broken and I drank in His forgiveness. He made a home in my heart, and He has stayed.

He entrusts any of us, who love Him, with the most challenging ventures, at home or elsewhere. He can stir us in prayer, to ask for what looks impossible. He determines the outcome of our days as we commit them to Him. Sometimes the way ahead is clear, on other days it is simply small steps of faith that we take to see if we are on the right track.

Whether in clarity or puzzlement we can be certain that Jesus is right there with us. He knows our frame, our limits. He is in His Word, His Spirit indwells us, and He is eager to fill us afresh with His empowering, sustaining grace each day as we ask.

He knows the way we take. He hearkens to our prayers, spoken or simply yearned for, and answers in His exquisite, carefully detailed wisdom even if we cannot always fully understand for now.

In some episodes of these accounts, I had to be intentionally vague or indirect in what I wrote in order to protect those with whom I was engaging. It requires reading between the lines in parts. Certain details of heavenly breakthrough had to be left out altogether to ensure someone's safety. Be assured that wherever the Word of God was shared, it raised curiosity and in instances, by God's working power, led to an intense search for more on who He is in Christ. At rare moments it was met with outright scorn or fear. I don't know the final outcome of some of the encounters, nor the fruit of my prayers for those I would not see again, but that is God's prerogative to reveal.

One report since leaving the refugee town, is that many, many people have come to Christ. Some are suffering intense rejection from their families. In joy I can tell that the one who taught me in her kitchen the names in her mother-tongue for ingredients, and let me peel an apple for her, is now the Lord's child.

Her own daughter, who worked the dough so skilfully for her mother, has sadly passed away. After marrying and carrying a child to full-term she did not survive. The snow was too deep for the ambulance to get through for medical care of her. She and her little one are with the Lord.

Some families have suffered more than we can imagine. I will forever treasure her crocheted lace edging on my dupatta worn for Joya's wedding. I still recall her radiant smile as I sat with her on the floor with the flames of the primus firing a delicious stew.

Some sorrows have no simple answer, except that God grieves too. He knows our pain.

He makes perfect what we experience as imperfect.

As I have brought this book to completion, I recall an elderly gentleman I met in 2006, before this story began. I was in St. Andrew's cathedral in Sydney in a Healing Service. I had come because I needed comfort. My father had died, my sister and then my mother had passed away, all within a confined number of years. All were now wonderfully in glory, but each left a deep space in my life. I wondered what my life held from thereon. I asked for prayer. The elderly man greeted me with a gentle smile and offered to pray. I stood by one of the pillars of the cathedral and shared with him my empty heart. He put his hand on my shoulder and prayed. At the close of our encounter he said to me very intently:

"In praying for you I have a sense God has something for you to do. I think you will be surprised"

I accepted his confidence and wondered. I think of that elderly brother in Christ. Fourteen years on I could tell him, I now know what God had in mind, and yes it was a surprise. He entrusted to me, ventures I could never have imagined.

Whatever struggle or triumph has been our experience, we have a place in sharing the news of the kingdom, in our own unique way. What might seem an insignificant conversation to us, can be critical in God's plan for the one who listens. We are flawed and still vulnerable, but God is strong and powerful. Christ in us, and our lives hidden in Him is our confidence. It is His story and His life He imparts to us as a living Christ.

I can bear witness that God our Father is lovingly and wisely mindful of each one of us.

He has given us His Word and the Holy Spirit to walk with Him in obedience if we are willing. Even in the midst of overwhelming pain, misunderstanding, or bewildering disappointments, by grace He is able to give us glimpses of heaven, couched in the quietness of trust. Trust to see His hand at work in our everyday lives and those around us.

"But we have this treasure in earthen vessels, that the excellence of the power may be of God and not of us."
2 Corinthians 4:7 (NKJV)

ACKNOWLEDGEMENTS

To set out on these journeys I was supported by my trusting family.

Close friends stood with me and for me when going on repeated mission was contested.

When I needed financial assistance my own family and church families gave so willingly.

For those who prayed for me, I cannot thank you enough. When perplexed, your prayers were as a protective cloak around me. The Lord assured me of His presence and your companionship.

For those I confided in for direction and who helped me take the one next step in front of me, thank you. I needed your wisdom of experience.

To the one who gave me fresh courage when I had little strength left, thank you.

For the two organisations who facilitated three of these trips, I am also very grateful.

To the one who gave me professional counselling on my return home, thank you. You helped me heal. To no longer be weighed down by grim memories was a deep freedom.

For those who helped bring this story to print, a huge thank you. It would not have happened without you.

Any reward, any joy from these trips is to be shared with each one of you who contributed in so many ways. I am deeply grateful to God for you.

All Things Bright & Beautiful

All things bright and beautiful
All creatures great and small
All things wise and wonderful
The Lord God made them all.

Each little flower that opens
Each little bird that sings
He made their glowing colours
He made their tiny wings.

The purple-headed mountains
The river running by
The sunset and the morning
That brightens up the sky.

The cold wind in the winter
The pleasant summer sun
The ripe fruits in the garden
God made them every one.

He gave us eyes to see them
And lips that we might tell
How great is God Almighty
Who has made all things well.

All things bright and beautiful
All creatures great and small
All things wise and wonderful
The Lord God made them all.

By Cecil F. Alexander. Published 1848

All Things Bright and Beautiful in the Rahim Yar Khan Schooll

A grandmother in the flood zone of Pakistan

Meeting up again with the women who whispered
the word Jesus when we first met.

The Muslim landlord come to pay his respect and
condolences to his tenant farmers.

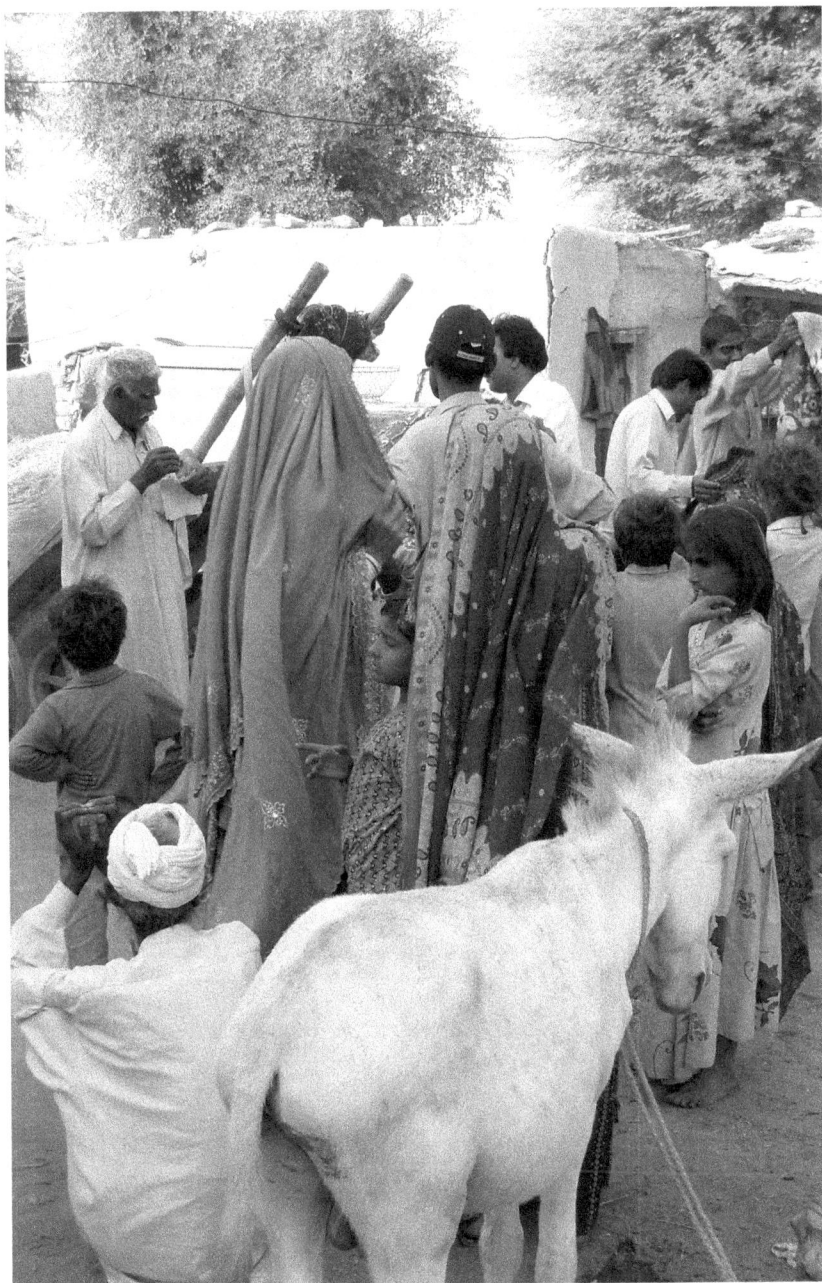

A Christian pastor distributing clothes to flood victims

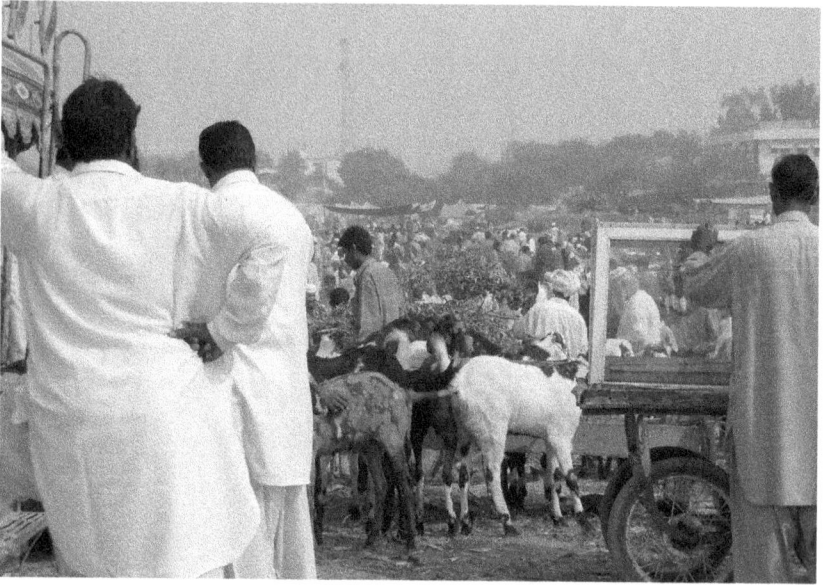
A livestock sale for Eid in Khaipur, Pakistan

An English student in Islamabad over whom there was great joy.

The mountains surrounding Quetta, Western Pakistan

Kumiko in the Christian Hospital

With an Autistic child in the Christian Hospital, Quetta.

The road to Hazaratown, Western Pakistan

Joya's mother and Marion

Joya and his bride Rahima with Joya's sister Marzia in the background

Guladahm the crochet-lacemaker with deft fingers.

Descent into Kabul, Afghanistan across the Hindu Kush mountain range.

The marketpace in Mazar-e-Sharif, Northern Afghanistan

Jemeel in the International Assistance mission, Afghanistan

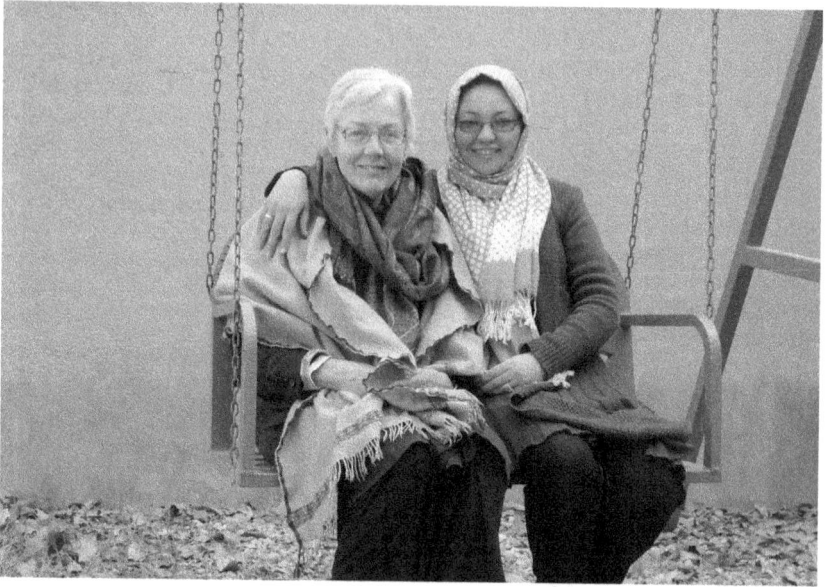

The English Teacher with Marion at the Women's
College in Mazar-e-Sharif in Afghanistan

English students on the last day of term, Women's College, Mazar-e-Sharif

Students met me with a welcome on arriving in China

English students Samuel & his wife Sarah, with Mako in the centre.
Mako and Marion met in the cold morning street.

The last evening meal in China

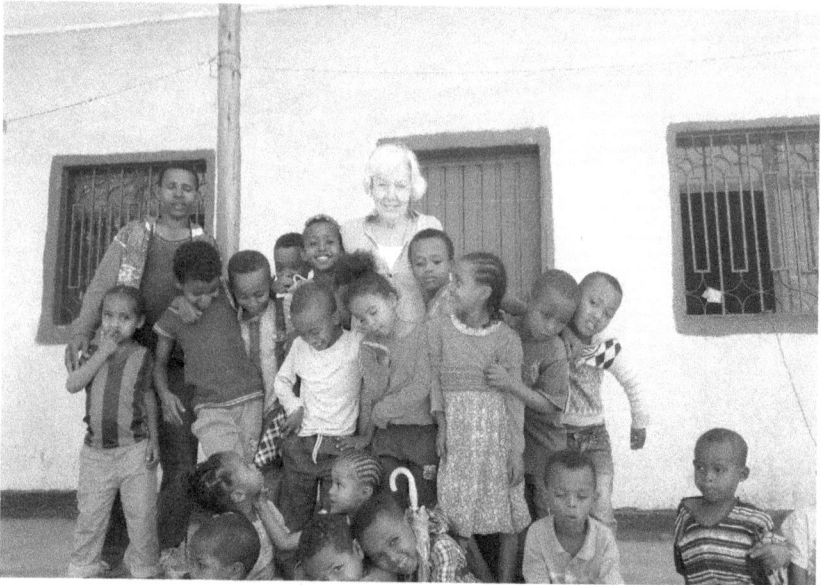

The children in the Infants' School in Gesuba, in
the Southern mountains of Ethiopia.

Teaching children in the school in Gesuba, Ethiopia

Our team in the school in Gesuba.
Caleb, Almaz, Natasia our evening guest, and David

Ephraim, our trusty Ethiopian interpreter in Gesuba, Ethiopia.

Gentle and persuasive hospitality to the aroma of home-grown, home-roasted and home-brewed coffee in Gesuba, Southern Ethiopia.

Dusk in Gesuba, in the mountains of Southern Ethiopia